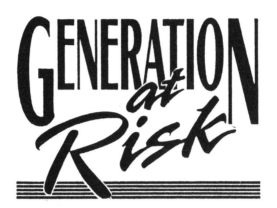

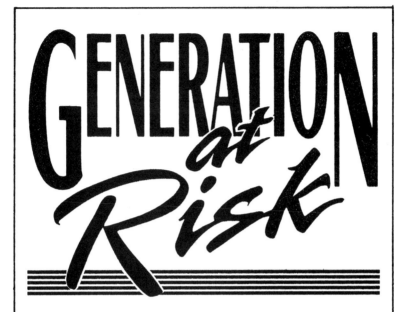

GENERATION at Risk

What Legacy Are the Baby-Boomers Leaving Their Kids?

FRAN SCIACCA

MOODY PRESS

CHICAGO

ISBN: 0-8024-2949-1

1 2 3 4 5 6 Printing/LC/Year 95 94 93 92 91

Printed in the United States of America

For Ben, Geoff, Heather, and Havilah.
May you never be put at risk.

CONTENTS

Part I
Why Is a Generation at Risk?

Prosperity, hope, and noble ideals. In their youth, an optimistic, cheerful generation known as the Baby Boomers seemed to have it all. But what has happened to their children? The present youth generation is at great emotional, social, and spiritual risk. Teenagers are eight times more likely to attempt suicide than the teens of twenty years ago, and today's teens account for almost one-third of all abortions. Can the plight of the youth generation be traced to the choices of the previous generation?

Part II
Age of Aquarius . . . Or Eve of Destruction?

Disillusionment. Shattered dreams of peace, justice, and universal love would sour the Baby Boom generation. Those broken dreams caused Baby Boomers to question and ultimately reshape traditional moral values.

Part III
The American Church: A House Built on Sand?

The Christian church, seeking respect from the larger culture, slowly has shifted from the absolutes of Scripture to the standards of the culture itself. Now the church's teens have begun to absorb the values of the larger youth culture as well.

Part IV
Can the Foundations Be Restored?

The biblical and moral foundations of society can be restored if Christians return to an essential perspective, one based on accepting our identity as followers of Jesus Christ. We can salvage the generation at risk only if we return to a biblical worldview and an authentic faith. The author shows us how.

ACKNOWLEDGMENTS

The release of a book is much like the production of a play. Particularly this one, because it has been revised and expanded. Though the author's name appears in bold print on the cover, a host of unnamed or unnoticed others have contributed to the effort.

I am indebted to the students at the Colorado Springs Christian School. The burden to write *Generation at Risk* is largely a product of their questions, pain, failures, and successes. They gave me a reason to write. And they faithfully prayed for me during the time I was off-campus rewriting *Generation*. I'd also like to express my gratitude to my long-time friend and mentor Dan Rich, who six years ago saw potential in me at a time when I didn't. He introduced me to World Wide Publications, the original publisher of the book, and continues to be a source of encouragement and counsel.

I'd like to thank those at World Wide Publications who were responsible to varying degrees for the original book. In particular, my thanks to Steve Griffith, who saw potential in the idea, and to DeWayne Herbrandson who agreed to take the "risk" of publishing the first version of *Generation at Risk*. And Bill Deckard, my faithful editor-become-friend, whose meticulous concern for detail and authenticity kept me focused and encouraged throughout the arduous process of translating what was in my head and computer onto paper. The first edition of this book became a second shadow for him, following him home at nights and on weekends. I marvel at his dedication to me and this project. I am especially grateful for your efforts, Bill.

The composition, editing, production, and marketing of any book are essential for its success. Yet, there are four individuals whose input was actually more essential. Without them, *Generation at Risk* would not exist, because its author would not be the man he has become. Twenty-one years ago, amidst the confusion and conflict of the sixties, a young man took time to share the love of Christ and the message of salvation with me. Without his commitment to the Lord and willingness to look beyond the abrasive, abusive, and vulgar exterior that characterized a young college student named Fran Sciacca, I most likely would have become merely another casualty of the decade. Wally Schultz showed me what it means to trust Jesus Christ. That eventful day in April of 1970 changed my personal history for eternity. He showed me the way to faith. Today, over two decades later, he still stands as an example of a man who truly has a Christian mind and heart.

Pastor Vivian Laird taught me what it means to know God and value people. To this day, no man has made a greater lasting impact on my life. He showed me what it means to be in love with God.

The late Francis A. Schaeffer taught me how to think as a Christian. The imprint of his outlook and understanding of the Christian worldview is present on virtually every page of this book. His books adorn my shelves with pride, and I can only hope that this work can have a fraction of the impact on others' lives that his works have had on mine.

Finally, there is one person who walked and talked me through the concepts of this book. My wife, Jill, helped *Generation at Risk* evolve from a one-hour talk on a blackboard to what it has become today. She challenged me about my conclusions when I wanted to "wrap up" an idea, always bringing new possibilities to bear on my sometimes hasty judgments. It is more than a mere formality to say that, without Jill, this book would not exist. Her constant prayers, consistent encouragement, and incredible sacrifice cannot go unnoticed. She has been my best friend and most faithful support for nearly seventeen years and has believed in me at times when I no longer believed in myself. In the words of a popular song, she has been the wind beneath my wings. I love you, Jill.

INTRODUCTION

When a key item on the agenda at a state teachers' convention is a debate on whether to install condom vending machines in high school restrooms, one has to conclude that American culture is in trouble. A serious complication of that trouble is the fact that most people are unaware of the nature and degree of our culture's problems. Nor are they aware of the source of those problems, much less what needs to be done about them.

This lack of understanding is as prevalent among evangelical Christians as it is in secular society. I am convinced that the church has had decreasing success in protecting its youth from modern culture because it does not recognize the degree of its own association with and patronage of that culture.

Generation at Risk is a confrontational book. It is intended to confront readers with the seriousness of the present crisis among youth; to document the monumental contribution made to that crisis by the parents of these youth, the so-called "Woodstock generation"; and to call the church to act decisively in responding to this crisis.

WHAT THIS BOOK ISN'T

Someone has wisely said that the smallest package in the world is someone wrapped up in himself. This often seems true of those of us born between 1946 and 1964. We are the "baby boom" generation, which seems never to tire of talking and writing about itself. The last few years have spawned countless books by or about the "boomers," as the much celebrated sixties has enjoyed a series of twenty-year anniversaries. *Generation at Risk* is not merely one of those books. Nonetheless, when you consider that one out of three Americans fits the boomer species, discussion of such a dominant portion of the populace could not be totally absent from a book about our times.

Generation at Risk is not a sociological or historical treatise on the spiritual state of the nation. If you are interested in detailed, scholarly analyses of our times, let me suggest *Idols for Destruction*, by Herbert Schlossberg; *The Death of Ethics in America*, by Cal Thomas; *Against the Night*, by Charles Colson; and *Evangelicalism: The Coming Generation*, by J. D. Hunter. These works (listed in the bibliography) deal in detail with the present state of educational, spiritual, and moral affairs in the United States.

This book does not attempt to be a definitive evaluation of the decade of the sixties, even though it examines it in significant detail as the background to today's youth crisis. There are already more books in print about the sixties decade than it warrants, many of them the work of nostalgia merchants who seem to have lost their reason somewhere between Berkeley and Woodstock. Two books on the sixties counterculture that are intellectually sound and honest are *The Destructive Generation*, by Peter Collier and David Horowitz, and *The Dust of Death*, by Os Guinness.

Generation at Risk does not claim to be an exhaustive treatise on rock music, even though it does discuss in some detail the impact of contemporary music on American life and values. Because this discussion of music is purely illustrative of larger cultural themes, a great deal of the history of contemporary music is absent. For instance, there is virtually no mention of the variety of black artists, songs, and styles that influenced the more visible white music. And only passing reference is made to the Beatles even though their pilgrimage from classic rock-and-roll to Eastern metaphysical themes is a miniature paradigm of the entire youth culture.

Finally, this book is not a simplistic analysis of, or a panacea for, the ills of our nation and the church. In fact, it may generate more questions than it answers. That would please me immensely! Evangelical Christians have a tendency to apply simplistic solutions to complex social and spiritual issues. *Generation at Risk* does not purport to have the answer, or the program, for turning the tide. However, if it can help in diminishing the damage from the storm, it will be a success.

What It Is

Generation at Risk is an examination of the historical-cultural context in which the church finds herself in the twilight of the twentieth century. There is much written today about the condition of the church, especially its youth. A common error is to try to interpret this moment in history without a serious discussion of its intellectual and social ancestry. We cannot succeed in understanding the present times and people unless we consider the legacy of what has gone before.

Another youth book, offering specialized information on one or more youth problems, is not needed. A host of books already exist that outline the social, economic, and spiritual plagues ravishing America's youth. What is needed is solid help in understanding this generation. This book tries to paint the "big picture"—the social and historical context out of which the present generation has emerged, the cultural frame that has shaped their thinking, values, and outlook.

Rather than being a how-to book, this will be more of a "how come" analysis—an inquiry into what was responsible for putting the present generation at risk, and what we can do about it.

Generation at Risk was written especially for those within the circumference of the Judeo-Christian ethic, but the truths it contains have immediate application for anyone who works or lives with, or simply wants to understand, the rising generation.

As king-in-exile, David was seeking to form an army to defend himself against the treachery of his son Absalom. He gathered men from the tribes of Israel who could contribute various skills to the effort. One group in particular was the tribe of Issachar. These men "had understanding of the times, to know what Israel ought to do," (1 Chronicles 12:32; RSV*).

Today there is a desperate need for Christian men and women who have "understanding of the times" and know what ought to be done. Though we boast to have the eternal truth of God, ironically we seem to be the last to know what is happening around us and why. It is my prayer that this book will provide an enhanced understanding of the times— who we are, how we got this way, and some suggestions for healing what is weak and strengthening what is sound.

SEEING THE NEED

Although this book was born in the seventies while I was working as an environmental chemist, its gestation began during my years of growing up as a part of the boomer generation, my experiences as a rock and folk rock musician, and my eventual disillusionment with the sixties ideology and conversion to Christ. The book was nursed and nourished by the hundreds of young Christians who have populated my world for thousands of hours during a decade of teaching. Consequently, though I am not a sociologist and

Revised Standard Version.

this is not the result of an academic study, it is based on an exposure to the soul of the next generation of Christians that few of my peers have been privileged to experience.

I have taught high school Bible in one of our nation's larger Christian day schools for ten years. Our school receives students from nearly 120 local churches in a city of more than three hundred thousand. The socioeconomic and theological groups present in our student body were representative of the Christian community at large, both locally and nationally. I have made it a personal goal to become intimately acquainted with my students. I have counseled and ministered to them through the rites of adolescence.

But as the years have gone by, I have found myself becoming immersed in an ever-growing swamp of complex emotional, moral, and domestic problems. Families are deteriorating, and my students' belief in the inviolability of the marriage vow is deteriorating as well. My conversations with parents have unearthed an alarming degree of biblical illiteracy and a secularization of values. More and more parents are abdicating their responsibility in training their child and instilling values, arguing that teachers should train their children instead. In the process, my responsibilities have increased dramatically. And my insight into the true condition of evangelical Christianity has been greatly enhanced.

This book is not, however, an exposé on some alleged deterioration of Christian education. Our school remains an excellent institution. Its staff and faculty are deeply committed to Jesus Christ, to a high view of the Bible, and to the imperative of fully integrated, Bible-centered education. The Christian school, like its secular counterpart, is merely a reflection of the homes from which its students come. Blaming impersonal institutions has always been preferable to admitting personal complicity and guilt. Christian schools rarely corrupt Christian children. Of that I am certain.

Part 1

WHY IS A GENERATION AT RISK?

*There is a battle for the hearts and minds of teenagers to-
day. I am more convinced of it than I've ever been before,
that if we lose the battle for the minds of our young people,
the entire understanding of the Judeo-Christian ethic
which was so predominant from the foundation of this
country to the present day, can be lost in one generation.*

Dr. James Dobson
"Focus on the Family"

*Who have I seen who looks after the wind,
Laughing and dancing at his play?
Who have I seen who looks after the wind,
The frolicking wind, every day?*

*Who have I seen who looks after the clouds,
Moving so slowly in their flight?
Who have I seen who looks after the clouds,
From morning to noon, and from noon to night?*

*Who have I seen who looks after this world,
This world with its domes and shining halls?
Who have I seen who looks after this world?
I haven't seen anyone, no one at all.*

Sarah, age nine

1

GENERATION AT RISK

My high school students had asked me to do a lot of strange things over the previous eight years. But that day as I stood outside the door of the girls' restroom, I sensed that I was about to step into a totally new adventure. The voice on the other side of the door begged me to enter. Taking a deep breath, I pulled the door open and walked in.

The horrified look on Kari's face stopped me cold. She sat on the floor, cuddling the crumpled frame of another girl, a new freshman. Kari's eyes pleaded with me to be calm. I was. In fact, I was stunned. On the floor next to Kari's shoe was a small pool of blood. She opened her free hand to reveal a single-edged razor blade and then motioned with her eyes to the shaking mass of adolescence in her embrace. Kari's other hand was clasped tightly around the girl's lower arm. And as she slowly released her grip, I saw a gaping slash in the girl's wrist.

I quietly slipped out, ran to the office, and jerked our principal away from a conversation he was engaged in. I told him we had a suicide attempt in the upstairs girls' restroom. Quickly but discreetly he called 911, then sent our guidance counselor, a woman of experience and compassion, to the scene. Meanwhile, I went into his office and promptly fell apart!

In my eight years of teaching, I thought I had seen it all. My own past had been tainted with drug and alcohol abuse, immorality, and deceit. I had been a professional rock musician for nearly seven years. As I told students over the years, I had "been to the sewer and back" before becoming a Christian. I prided myself for being able to relate in a constructive way to my students' shortcomings and sin. But a suicide attempt during school? This was too much! However, before the school year ended, I would be drawn into two more such incidents.

Our school is probably one of the best Christian schools in the nation. With an enrollment of nearly nine hundred, we have a godly and caring faculty with a genuine vision to help our student body cultivate a Christian faith that is theologically conservative yet realistic. And most of our students are godly young people from stable, Christ-centered homes. But what was happening to these students? What was happening in our school?

This book is about two generations, one well into adulthood and the other still approaching it. It is a book about America and her children; about our past and their future. But it has much to do with our future too, because what remains for us will largely be delimited by what becomes of the present youth generation. This rising generation may very well be the most pivotal group in the history of the church in America, perhaps even of America itself. And I believe that this generation is a generation at risk.

We are justly alarmed by the fact that "in two decades the rate of teen suicide attempts has gone from ten out of 1000 to eight out of 100"[1] (an eightfold increase). And teenagers account for nearly one-third of all abortions in the United States.[2] One out of four high school age children in America drop out of school, never to return.[3] Gang violence is at an all time high. An increasingly common scene in many American public high schools is a young girl dropping off her infant at an on-site day-care center so she can attempt to finish school. "Crack babies" and "AIDS babies" are terms none of us knew when we were growing up, but they are a familiar part of the vocabulary of most youth today.

To make matters worse, the primary institution that historically provided some sense of stability amid rapid social change—the family—has experienced a serious dismantling. The American family has become nearly undefinable. It has become a conglomerate of single parents, step-parents, step-siblings, and abandoned children. It is more than statistically fascinating that "today more people are single or remarried than are part of an intact family. We have become a nation of step-relating individuals."[4] For a growing majority of America's youth, little remains that is constant, whereas that which is indifferent and hostile continues to grow.

Many of us in the "older generation" stand perplexed by the actions of young people today. Most of us have some recollection of destructive behavior in our own pasts. Yet we grew up. We moved on. By contrast, a growing number of young people today seem prisoners in time, marooned in their sense of despair. We find ourselves wavering somewhere between compassion, confusion, and criticism.

Some adults are tired of what appears to be a constant pandering to youth. They insist that the emotional migration from child to adult has never been easy and has always been characterized by conflict between generations. Even Socrates in the sixth century B.C. seemed to attest to this universal truth:

> Youth today loves luxury. They have bad manners, contempt for authority, no respect for older people, and talk nonsense when they should work. Young people do not stand up any longer when adults enter the room. They contradict their parents, talk too much in company, guzzle their food, lay their legs on the table, and tyrannize their elders.[5]

Many adults will say that young people should "pull themselves up by their own bootstraps," like they had to do. A nationally syndicated columnist recently wrote a scathing editorial in which he accused today's youth of being a bunch of whiners. He told his youthful readers that they are the "best-fed, best-clothed, and best-educated generation in American history," and then went on to give his reasons for not feeling sorry for them. His message was basically, "Shut up, shape up, or ship out!" His status as an ivory-tower journalist afforded him the luxury of dismissing the plight of today's youth with a few artful strokes of his pen.

Those of us who have worked and lived in the midst of today's youth realize that it is a bit more complicated than that. In fact, thirty-year veteran youth worker Mike Yaconelli is convinced that youth have changed so dramatically that unless youth workers, churches, and organizations that work with the rising generation change, they will be incapable of reaching American youth in the nineties.[6]

An adult reader from Georgia recently wrote to Ann Landers voicing his disgust over the inability of today's youth to pull their lives together. Essentially, he said they don't know what a difficult life is. An insightful and articulate sixteen-year-old reader responded. The pain in her letter is exceeded only by its accuracy:

> Dear Ann Landers:
> The reader signed "Georgia" who lived through the Depression and described how hard it was to be a teenager in the thirties, said kids today have an easy time of it compared to teens in his day. You said you couldn't argue with him. Well, I can.
> Let me ask your generation a few questions:

Are your parents divorced? Almost every one of my friends comes from a broken home.
Were you thinking about suicide when you were 12?
Did you have an ulcer when you were 16?
Did your best friend lose her virginity to a guy she went out with twice?
You may have had to worry about VD, but did you have to worry about AIDS?
Did your classmates carry knives and guns?
How many kids in your class came to school regularly drunk, stoned or high on drugs?

Did any of your friends have their brains fried from using PCP?

What percentage of your graduating class also graduat-
ed from a drug and alcohol rehabilitation center?

Did your school have armed security guards in the halls?

Did you ever live in a neighborhood where the sound of
gunfire at night was "normal"?

You talk a lot about being dirt poor and having no money. Since when does money mean happiness? The kids at
school who have the expensive cars and designer clothes are
the most miserable.

When I am your age, Georgia, I won't do much looking
back, I'll just thank God that I survived.

Other Side of the Story in Indianapolis.[7]

Her letter is a résumé of the despondency of the rising
generation and the misunderstanding or indifference of our
own. Hers is a generation at risk.

They are not at risk because of global warming, sexually
transmitted diseases, substance abuse, or teen pregnancy, as
serious as all these problems are. What we label the drug
problem, the teen pregnancy problem, and the host of other
problems of youth are merely the symptoms of a much larger, deep-rooted, and serious dilemma. Today's youth are at
risk simply because they have no satisfactory reason to live.
This is just as true of Christian young people as of those outside the influence of Christianity.

But before we can understand the present generation
and discover how they became a generation at risk, we need
to go back in time. For it is there that most of the puzzle
pieces are to be found. In the words of T. S. Eliot:

Wisdom is only gained in two ways, and well gained only
through both: a study of human nature through history, the
actions of men in the past and the best that they have written
and thought, and a study through observation and experience
of the men and women about us as we live.[8]

NOTES

1. Josh McDowell and Dick Day, *Why Wait?* (San Bernardino, Calif.: Here's Life, 1987), p. 31.
2. Josh McDowell, "Where Our Youth Are Today," Focus on the Family, audio cassette CS334.
3. "High School Dropouts: Renewed Attention to an Old Problem," *Youthworker Update*, December 1986, p. 2.
4. "A Nation of Stepfamilies," *Youthworker Update*, December 1986, p. 6.
5. Quoted in *Youthworker Update*, January 1988, p. 8.
6. "Complex Problems of Teenagers Spur Young Life to Life," *Colorado Springs Gazette Telegraph*, January 6, 1990, D2. Yaconelli states in strong terms that the underlying need in the lives of young people is for someone they respect and love to spend time with them. My teaching experience confirms that his conclusion applies to Christian young people as much as to those from non-Christian homes.
7. Ann Landers, "Some Teens Face Difficult Problems," *Colorado Springs Gazette Telegraph*, December 15, 1989, E6. Reprint permission granted by Ann Landers and Creators Syndicate.
8. From a speech to a meeting of Anglo-Catholic sociologists, 1933. Quoted by Russell Kirk in "Historical Consciousness and the Preservation of Culture," *The World & I*, January 1989, pp. 491-501.

It was the best of times, it was the worst of times, it was the age of wisdom, it was the age of foolishness, it was the epoch of belief, it was the epoch of incredulity, it was the season of Light, it was the season of Darkness, it was the spring of hope, it was the winter of despair, we had everything before us, we had nothing before us, we were all going direct to Heaven, we were all going direct the other way.

Charles Dickens
A Tale of Two Cities

2

A Tale of Two Generations

Dickens's words are an apt description of the decade that has been fondly christened "the fifties." It was the closest to national schizophrenia the United States has ever come. The postwar economic machine, fueled by the war effort, was just beginning to spew out an avalanche of goods and services. "Peace, Progress, and Prosperity" would become President Eisenhower's appealing reelection slogan.

But in another part of the American psyche, a political fear bordering on paranoia was writhing and twisting, especially in the minds of the young who grew up within the perimeter of the Hula Hoop® and in the shadow of The Bomb. Germany had surrendered in May 1945, followed by Japan that August. The war and its impact was still a vivid memory in American households. The memory hardly had a chance to fade when the Soviet Union tested its first atomic bomb in 1949, forever dispelling the hope that another war would never happen. And beginning in June 1950, our unpopular involvement in Korea was a sharp reminder that war or its threat was a given fact of life.

In 1951, the first publicized bomb shelter was built by Mrs. Ruth Calhoun in Los Angeles. On November 1, 1952, the United States tested its first hydrogen bomb at Eniwetok in the Marshall Islands. Russia tested its first H-bomb in 1953, followed the next year by our second H-bomb test. In November, Soviet dictator Nikita Khrushchev pounded his shoe on a table in the United Nations General Assembly and shouted, "We will bury you!"

In the midst of this frenzied search for power, Albert Einstein made a frightening prediction: "Radioactive poisoning of the atmosphere and hence annihilation of any life on earth has been brought within the range of technical possibilities."[1]

On October 4, 1957, Russia stunned America by placing into orbit Sputnik, a man-made 184-pound satellite. They followed this feat with two more launches, one of which contained a live animal. The space race had begun.

It would be both naive and foolish to minimize the impact this had on those growing up in the fifties. In the back of their minds was the gnawing question: "What does life hold for us?" During the sixties, this question would evolve into: "What is the meaning of life?"

But these dark forebodings were not the sum total of the national psyche in the fifties. In 1952, Dwight Eisenhower and Richard Nixon were elected to the executive offices. Their passion was to maintain the economic boom the war had created. Regarding the Eisenhower era, Charles Colson notes:

> After fifteen years of depression and war, unemployment and rationing, Americans were determined to make up for lost time—and as the years went on, times were good. . . . For the first time in history nearly everyone could afford their own home; millions of returning veterans went to college on the GI Bill; business boomed. Eisenhower's 1956 reelection theme, "Peace, Progress, and Prosperity," captured the mood of the nation.[2]

EVERYTHING BEFORE US

Most Americans enjoyed the burst of economic prosperity. I recall my father, a typical member of the blue-collar working class, telling me that he wanted me to have all the things he never had, not the least of which was a proper education. The lifestyle of the "middle class" enjoyed geometric growth during Eisenhower's years in the White House, in everything from hot dogs to encyclopedias.

GROWTH DURING EISENHOWER ERA[3]

ITEM	1950 (millions)	1960 (millions)	% increase
lawn & porch furniture sales	$53.6	$145.2	270
hot dog production (lb.)	750	1050	140
gin production (gal.)	6	19	317
vodka production (gal.)	0.1	9	9,000
encyclopedia sales	$72	$300	417
musical instrument sales	$86	$149	173
Little Leagues	776*	5,700*	735
Girl Scouts & Brownies	1.8	4.0	222
forest campers	1.5	6.6	440
bowling alleys	0.5	1	222

*raw number

The birth of the backyard barbeque spurred hot dog production and lawn furniture sales, and the growing popularity of cocktail parties prompted consumption of alcoholic beverages. These two phenomena are good indices of America's increased emphasis on leisure, as opposed to the previous decade's necessary preoccupation with survival and hard work. America learned to play in the fifties, but unfortunately she also seemed to forget how to think.

During the Eisenhower era there was a pendulum swing toward accumulating goods. "It was the Twenties prosperity over again, but less frenetic and more secure, with a far wider social spread. . . . The Fifties was the decade of affluence, a word popularized by the fashionable economist J. K. Galbraith in his 1958 best seller, *The Affluent Society.*"[4]

People eventually closed up their bomb shelters and settled down to enjoy the recent entertainment novelty—television. While politicians carried on the cold war, most Americans were watching the escapades of desperados on "Gunsmoke" and "Have Gun, Will Travel." The marital antics of "The Honeymooners," the model family on "Leave It to Beaver," and the unbelievable adventures of a dog called "Lassie" entertained young and old alike.

In 1950, 3.1 million homes had televisions. By 1955 the number had risen to 32 million. By the end of the decade, the average American family watched six hours of television per day, prompting columnist Harriet Van Horne to suggest, "Our people are becoming less literate by the minute. . . . As old habits decline, such as reading books and thinking thoughts, TV will absorb their time. By the twenty-first century our people doubtless will be squint-eyed, hunch-backed, and fond of the dark."[5]

This national euphoria is best illustrated, however, in the dominant music at the beginning of the era, "pop." This music style was basically a slightly modified carryover of the music of the forties, which was characteristically labeled "mood" music. From 1950 to 1955, pop artists like Patti Page, Brenda Lee, Harry Belafonte, Pat Boone, and Bing Crosby filled American homes with their crooning.

THE WINDS OF CHANGE

Life was great—for the adults. But what about the youth of America, the first generation to grow up after the advent of nuclear power? How were *they* responding to this new prosperity? How were they handling America's schizophrenic attempt to believe it was the best of times while fearing that it was the worst of times?

The young people of the fifties responded in three different ways to the materialism of the adult middle class. At first glance these responses seem unrelated, yet to some degree all were direct results of the adult preoccupation with "things."

The first response occurred among the urban poor. The decade between 1950 and 1960 saw an astonishing rise in violent urban gangs. In New York City, from 1955 to 1956, murders of teens rose 26 percent, auto theft rose 36 percent, and the possession of dangerous weapons rose 92 percent.[6] Rival gangs staked off their "turf" and fought to protect it. In their book *Home of the Brave*, John Alexander Carroll and Odie Faulk indict TV as a prime causal factor in the rise of violence, in that it visually portrayed things the urban youth would never own or experience.[7] It was a steady carrot dangling in their faces. Their rebellion was against a larger culture in which they seemed to be *persona non grata*. And as generally is the case in a battle between "haves" and "have nots," their rebellion took the form of action.

As parasitic on social ills then as now, the entertainment industry made the urban gang phenomenon into money-making ventures. Films like *High School Confidential, Blackboard Jungle, Teenage Doll,* and *Wild One* romanticized teen violence. The urban unrest motif even found its way onto Broadway in the musical *West Side Story*.

Urban violence was one of the responses to "Peace, Progress, and Prosperity," as inner-city youth searched for a sense of identity in a culture that had loosed itself from a meaningful shore. But these gangs comprised a relatively small part of the boomer generation.

A second, even smaller response to this materialism occurred among a quasi-intellectual elite. On the East Coast, at Columbia University, a handful of disenchanted veterans and college dropouts began to drop out even further. In coffeehouses and "pads," they wrote and read poetry and indulged in an increasingly liberal attitude toward sex and drugs. They were the "beat generation," the name being an abbreviation of *beatitude*, according to their own sources.[8] The media cynically labeled them "beatniks," parroting the recent launch of *Sputnik* by the Russians. These first social drop-outs were not unpatriotic. In fact, many were war veterans. They were un-American only in the sense that they found our national description of life shallow and wanting, and found in it an excuse for an alternate lifestyle.

The beats of the fifties were politically passive, as exemplified by Jack Kerouac, one of their leading spokesmen:

> Recently Ben Hecht said to me on TV, "Why are you afraid to speak out your mind, what's wrong with this country, what is everybody afraid of?" Was he talking to me? And all he wanted me to do was speak out my mind AGAINST people, he sneeringly brought up Dulles, Eisenhower, the Pope, all kinds of people like that habitually he would sneer at with Drew Pearson, AGAINST the world he wanted, this is his idea of freedom, he calls it freedom. Who knows, my God, but that the universe is not one vast sea of compassion actually, the veritable holy honey, beneath all this show of personality and cruelty.[9]

The passive nature of the beats would contrast sharply with their mutant progeny, the "hippies," who had little in common with them other than a basic antipathy toward the American way of life.

Two other prominent figures in the beat movement were Allen Ginsberg and Gregory Corso. These and other gurus of the beat scene traveled widely, pronouncing their blessings in poetry and song to other "hip" souls. Their following consisted more of a series of philosophical oases than of any coherent movement. "Punctuating the interminable traveling with intermittent pauses for pot, mescaline, sex and booze, the Beats became a loose tribe of experiential nomads who forged an axis from Greenwich Village to Berkeley, with stops between in Denver, Michigan, colonies in North Beach and Venice West and outposts in Mexico, Tangiers and Paris."[10]

The beats would perhaps have remained scattered, clandestine huddles of nonconformists had it not been for the American media. Ginsberg's book *Howl*, released in 1957, was nearly banned in San Francisco until a judge ruled that it had "redeeming social importance." The trial brought the beats into the national eye and gave them some degree of social legitimacy. Jack Kerouac's novel *On the Road* was released in 1959 and became a national best-seller, no doubt partly due to the notoriety the media had given Ginsberg two years earlier. The word *beatnik* was soon a part of everybody's vocabulary, right along with Chevrolet and Ford. I vividly recall my parents going to costume parties dressed as beatniks, though they had never heard of Allen Ginsberg, much less his writings. The closest most of us had come to the beat generation was through the sensitive but scatterbrained beatnik Maynard G. Krebs on the "Dobie Gillis" television show.

What started out as a small group merely seeking to make a statement through their lifestyle became a permanent fixture in the intellectual genealogy leading toward the sixties. The message of the beats was "I see what's going on in middle-class America and I don't like it, so I won't participate. I'll drop out." Theirs was the rebellion of passive aggression—a rebellion of identity. The beat movement, although temporary in form, would haunt American culture in the next decade. For in it a counterculture was born.

But what of the majority of middle-class children who were growing up in suburban homes, enjoying the "good life" of the fifties? What was happening to those who knew only about beatniks and nothing about the real-life beats, and whose only exposure to inner city gangs was seeing Marlon Brando in *Wild One*?

The attitude of many middle-class American youth was captured in another classic movie of the fifties. In *Rebel Without a Cause*, actor James Dean became an American folk hero. American young people were restless, but there was no focus, no clarity to their frustration. Best-selling author Stephen King, interviewed by Annie Gottlieb in her book *Do You Believe in Magic?*, pinpoints the inner agony Dean vicariously experienced for millions of fifties kids:

> I couldn't have been more than seven or eight years old when I saw Rebel Without a Cause, . . . And I still remember the intense emotional reaction I had. This kid comes home, and he's

been beaten up and treated badly, and Jim Backus, his father, says (simpering), "Well, let's have some milk, and then we'll make a list. That always helps me." And the kid says (screaming), "YOU'RE TEARING ME APAAART!" And it was like somebody opened a window inside my own heart. Somebody had said the truth.[11]

As with the young Stephen King, the good life of the fifties was offered to most American youth without any concern that perhaps they wanted something more meaningful. Annie Gottlieb accused the adult generation of substituting materialism for love.[12] Was there more to life than accumulating goods? What was life's meaning? These questions and a host of others floundered in the collective psyche of many middle-class kids. They sensed something was wrong somewhere, but the American youth in the fifties didn't know *what* was wrong. And even more important, no one talked about the questions—yet.

THE SOUND OF MUSIC

This free-floating uneasiness found a banner under which to gather in the most unexpected of places: a faltering attempt by adults to launch a new form of music.

In the early fifties, pop ruled the music world. It was the music *du jour* of every cocktail party in the land and occupied an unchallenged majority of all record sales. My childhood memories contain colorful recollections of the voices of Bing Crosby and Harry Belafonte drifting up to my room from the "rec room," where my folks and their friends were dancing the night away. But the winds of change were beginning to blow in music also.

Record companies were trying to create a new musical hybrid by mixing the vocal harmony of gospel music, the driving bass and drum beat of "boogie," and the themes of sex and romance from the blues. This new music was given the erotic handle of "rock-and-roll." Yet these early attempts by adult businessmen to break the pop monopoly failed. Early-

and mid-fifties releases of "Sh-Boom," by the Chords, and the now well-known "Rock Around the Clock," by Bill Haley and the Comets, huffed and puffed but couldn't blow the house of pop down.[13] A young, charismatic personality was needed to solicit the allegiance of the generation of "rebels without a cause" and wed them to this new genre. That catalyst was a twenty-one-year-old truck driver from Memphis named Elvis Presley.

Pop never knew what hit it! Elvis ("the Pelvis") put rock-and-roll on the radio and in the stores. Music has never recovered since 1956 when "Tutti Frutti," "Hound Dog," "Don't Be Cruel," and a seemingly endless list of other hits dominated the phonographs of America. Jackie Gleason, the well-known comedian of the day, said, "We'll survive Elvis. He can't last. I tell you flatly, he can't last."[14] Jackie was quite wrong, of course. Elvis captured the heart of young America. And even today, almost fifteen years after his death in 1977, people still want to believe he's alive.

Elvis opened the way for a multitude of other recording artists, both black and white. Rock-and-roll became the closest thing the United States has ever had to a state religion. Elvis provided the boomer generation with something distinctly their own—a new music. From 1957 on, the youth of America had their own medium, something that was to become essential for the spread of the ideology of the next decade. Rock-and-roll became the Western Union of American youth.

Rock-and-roll was more sexually explicit than pop, and therefore offensive to the parental generation, which only served to widen the gap of rebellion for those "without a cause." Yet rock-and-roll was certainly no cause. It was masterminded to sell records, not ideologies. When Elvis swung his hand across the strings, smacked his knees together, and convulsed, "A bop-bop-a-loom-op a-lop bop boom! Tutti Frutti, au rutti," he wasn't making a deep philosophical statement about life's meaning! Nonetheless, rock-and-roll was the single most important agent of cohesion for a generation looking for a reason to exist. It became a place of release for uneasiness and discontent.

As the fifties drew to a close, rebellion among the majority of middle-class kids occurred only in *attitude*. It was not yet a rebellion of *action*, as with the urban gangs. Nor were most middle-class youth seeking the sort of separate identity sought by the beats. Indeed, most people in the fifties, both young and old, were in agreement with "the system," the recognized institutions of authority such as church, home, state, and school. Noted demographer Cheryl Russell points out, "The allied victory in World War II gave Americans confidence in their institutions and leaders. The politicians and the military had achieved an enormous success, convincing Americans of the benevolence of authority—whether that authority was a politician, a minister, a psychiatrist, or a doctor."[15]

While times were good—at least better than they'd been for some time—there was among young people a growing attitude of presumed opposition to this good life (which they nonetheless enjoyed and exploited!). Middle-class young people, the very ones who would soon flood the campuses of America in the sixties, sensed there was something more to life than the emblems of success that characterized the Eisenhower era. Life was boring, as it inevitably becomes for those who have everything.

The kindling was ready, the smoke had begun to appear, but by the decade's end there was still no fire. That was about to change—forever. The best of times was about to be swallowed up by a worst of times that had nothing to do with the threat of war from without. America was about to encounter an enemy from within.

NOTES

1. Quoted in *This Fabulous Century*, vol. 6 (Alexandria, Va.: Time-Life, 1970), p. 31.
2. Charles Colson, *Kingdoms in Conflict* (Grand Rapids, Mich.: Zondervan/Morrow, 1987), p. 212.
3. *This Fabulous Century*, vol. 6, pp. 160-72.
4. Paul Johnson, *Modern Times* (New York: Harper & Row, 1983), p. 613.
5. *This Fabulous Century*, vol. 6, p. 176.
6. *This Fabulous Century*, vol.6, p. 234.
7. John Alexander Carroll and Odie B. Faulk, *Home of the Brave: A Patriot's Guide to American History* (Lanham, Md.: U. Press of America, 1984), p. 360.
8. *This Fabulous Century*, vol. 6, p. 88.
9. Jack Kerouac, quoted in *This Fabulous Century*, vol. 6, p. 88.
10. Os Guinness, *The Dust of Death* (Downers Grove, Ill.: InterVarsity, 1973), p. 81.
11. Annie Gottlieb, *Do You Believe in Magic?* (New York: Time, 1987), p. 28.
12. Ibid., p. 234.
13. It should be noted that although Haley's song was a number one hit on the charts in 1955, the number two song that year was "Ballad of Davy Crockett," followed by "Cherry Pink and Apple Blossom White." This indicates rock and roll was not yet in the mainstream. In 1956 and the years that followed, rock music controlled a growing portion of the record market.
14. *This Fabulous Century*, vol. 6, p. 145.
15. Cheryl Russell, *100 Predictions for the Baby Boom* (New York: Plenum, 1987), pp. 34-35. A statement Russell quotes from *Look* magazine suggests that "the system" was enjoying a broad consensus of support as late as 1965: "Americans today bear themselves like victory-laden champions. They've won their wars and survived their depressions. They are accustomed to meeting, and beating, tests. They are experienced pragmatists, buoyed by a system that works. And they believe in their managers" (Leonard Gross, "America's Mood Today," *Look*, June 29, 1965, p. 21).

The iceberg of tranquility that was Eisenhower was float-ing in a sea of disturbance, for prosperity was bringing more and yet more Americans into the upper middle class and causing them to advance idealistic—and unrealistic —demands. During the 1950s this growing band of self-styled intellectuals and self-proclaimed messiahs was mov-ing the country dramatically to the left, promoting hedonism, immorality, racial unrest, and worship of the young. Commercial television was coming of age, intensi-fying the unrest of the unproductive by making them aware of goods and services they had never before realized were to be had . . . liberal professors [were] preaching an elitist philosophy to unsophisticated, naive, idealistic students who believed them. While on the surface the 1950s were placid, underneath there was seething unrest that would explode into violence and drastic change in the 1960s.

John Alexander Carroll
Home of the Brave

3

LIFE IN CAMELOT

As a Roman Catholic youth who grew up in a small Wisconsin town, I can still recall the excitement that flooded our parochial school when we heard that a young Catholic president had just been elected. He was charming and witty, his wife seemed to be plucked from the pages of a storybook, and there were children in the White House! John F. Kennedy had indeed brought "Camelot" to America. As a child of ten, it never occurred to me that life would be radically different by the time I was twenty.

Life in 1960 was still good—or at least we were still enjoying it. By now "our" music was a permanent fixture in anything having to do with youth; it was the social axis around which our lives rotated. My own involvement in rock music escalated greatly during the sixties, beginning with playing bass for a popular rock band in high school and building to a zenith in college with a talented folk-rock group.

As the sixties began, its music reflected a worldview preoccupied with fun, and seemed to focus on three main themes: romance, cars, and surfing. There were more bands and solo artists than one could imagine, but the supergroup of the decade's early years was The Beach Boys. They wove all three dominant themes into a musical fantasy that appealed to any teenager with functioning hormones:

> In the sixties, when they were at the height of their original popularity, The Beach Boys propagated their own variant on the American dream, painting a dazzling picture of beaches, parties and endless summers, a paradise of escape into private as often as shared pleasures. . . .
> In surfing, The Beach Boys had hit upon a potent image. Leisure, mobility and privacy—it was the suburban myth transported to the Pacific Ocean . . . California—in 1963, it was the one place west of the Mississippi where everyone wanted to be. Rich and fast, cars, women, one suburban plot for everyone; a sea of happy humanity sandwiched between frosty mountains and toasty beaches, all an easy drive down the freeway.[1]

An abbreviated discography of the Beach Boys' singles illustrates the dominance of these themes, not to mention their vast appeal:[2]

A PARTIAL LIST OF BEACH BOYS SINGLES, 1962-1966

"Surfin'"	1962	"Do You Wanna Dance?"	1965
"Surfin' Safari"	1962	"Help Me Rhonda"	1965
"Surfin' U.S.A."	1963	"California Girls"	1965
"Surfer Girl"	1963	"Barbara Ann"	1966
"Little Deuce Coupe"	1963	"Sloop John B"	1966
"Fun, Fun, Fun"	1964	"Good Vibrations"	1966
"Dance, Dance, Dance"	1964		

Between 1963 and 1975, this powerful group churned out twenty-eight albums. Through their flights of fantasy, the Beach Boys did a great deal to perpetuate the image of what Jim Miller called an "uncomplicated suburban utopia." As an adolescent I was contemplating visions of bikinis (something relatively unheard of in the frigid hinterlands of Wisconsin) and making skateboards out of scrap lumber and broken roller skates—rather than studying social injustice or the conflict in Indochina. At the dawn of my teen years, the only black person I had ever seen was Hank Aaron when my Boy Scout troop took a bus trip to a Braves game in Milwaukee.

But a social conscience would soon awake in this generation, led by its musicians. As the youth culture scooped up records, an increasing number of young people decided that they too would become rock-and-roll stars. Guitar sales skyrocketed. As a result, almost overnight, the thoughts and feelings of American youth, rather than those dictated by the record company producers, began to become noticeable themes in music. The standard themes of teenage sexuality and adventure remained, but a new form of popular music began to encroach on the hallowed ground of rock. Folk music, or folk-rock, to be more precise, had a more thoughtful and penetrating message.

One of the pioneers of this new music was a young man from the Iron Range in Minnesota. Robert Zimmerman migrated east, changed his name to Bob Dylan, and became a household word to those of us now in our thirties and forties. He couldn't sing, but man could he write! The content of his songs totally eclipsed his lack of vocal talent. Consider the following description of Dylan and his music:

> He popped up out of nowhere, another unknown, unscrubbed face in Greenwich Village, and now, only two years later, he sits in the pantheon of the folk-music movement. His name is Bob Dylan, he is 22 years old, and his bewildered brown-blond hair trails off into uneven sideburns. . . . His singing voice scratches and shouts so jarringly that his success, at first, seems incredible. Yet his knack for stirring audiences is unmistakable, and it stems, mainly, from the words of the some 200 songs he has written, simple words that pounce upon the obvious—the inequalities, dangers, and deceits of the 1960s—and hammer them home.[3]

In some ways, Dylan was to the sixties what Elvis was to the fifties—an agent of cohesion. Yet, to fully appreciate the pathos of this music, we need to examine a few facts about the larger culture, which in many ways was responsible for its success.

CLOUDS ON THE HORIZON

Before Kennedy stepped over the threshold of the Oval Office to assume his duties as president, "Vietnam was already one of America's largest and costliest commitments anywhere in the world."[4] Eisenhower had deliberately refused to involve the United States in the battle over the Seventeenth Parallel during his own administration, but shortly before his retirement from public scrutiny, he conveniently commented: "The loss of South Vietnam would set in motion a crumbling process that could, as the process progressed, have grave consequences for us and for freedom."[5]

This idea would later be popularized as the "domino theory." In 1964, the North Vietnamese attacked U.S. destroyers in the Gulf of Tonkin, and the ensuing Tonkin Gulf Resolution gave President Lyndon Johnson the authority to escalate American involvement to full-scale war, which he did six months later, after the Vietcong Tet Offensive.

The Vietnam War was an issue that grew to be a cause in what would become known as "the movement" as the sixties decade progressed. Soon, groups like the Weathermen (the violent faction of the Students for a Democratic Society, or SDS) would be chanting, "Bring the war home," instead of, "Bring the boys home." In all its vagueness, Vietnam became a cause almost synonymous with the sixties. But Vietnam was only one cause for the rebels of the decade. Another focal point was the plight of black Americans.

In truth, the civil rights movement was considerably older than the anti-war movement, its visible origins dating back to the mid-fifties. As early as the mid-fifties, federal judges had ruled that segregation was unconstitutional in institutions of learning. But the dictum that "you can't legislate morality" was proved true. In 1957, Eisenhower had to send troops into Arkansas to force the governor to comply with desegregation orders. President Kennedy used the same tactic five years later in the case of James Meredith at the University of Mississippi.

By 1963, a black Baptist minister who advocated a non-violent approach to the civil rights issue had amassed an enormous following. In August of that year, two hundred thousand supporters gathered as Martin Luther King, Jr., delivered a speech at the Washington Monument. And "I have a dream" was permanently etched into the American consciousness. Dr. King was a charismatic organizer who brought a sense of solidarity to the civil rights cause. He had sympathetic supporters among a growing number of white college students as well as in the black community. Many whites participated in the effort to register black voters in the South in the early sixties, in what was known as the Mississippi Summer Project.[6]

In retrospect, these were some of the last days of genuine altruism in what was slowly becoming "the movement." The necessity of organization often has institutionalization as its unfortunate offspring. Altruism would soon be replaced by enterprise and excess.

Some in the black community were impatient with Dr. King's diplomatic style. They advocated a faster method of bringing "justice" to the ghetto. The civil rights movement turned intensely militant during the mid-sixties, with Huey Newton's Black Panther party leading the way. Older, less violent civil rights organizations, such as Stokely Carmichael's Student Nonviolent Coordinating Committee, began to lose their notoriety and clout as the Black Panthers and their white compatriots in the movement gained momentum and power.

Many sixties observers point to the assassination of President Kennedy in 1963 as the day the "militant/activist" sixties began and the age of passive innocence ended. By mid-decade, race riots and war protests had erupted in nearly sixty cities, killing 141 (mostly in the race riots) and injuring more than 4,500. The assassinations of Martin Luther King, Jr., and Bobby Kennedy in 1968 added more fuel to the fire. The catch phrase on buttons around college campuses had been "Give a Damn." But by the decade's end, "giving a damn had become a bitter, angry thing."[7]

Intensity and Commitment

The era had an almost hypnotic effect on those of us in college at the time. It was as if someone had actually followed Abbie Hoffman's half-serious suggestion to put LSD in the drinking water. My own brother was in 'Nam (soon to be seriously wounded by mortar fire), while I was skipping classes, mindlessly brandishing my black arm band, which I believed was evidence of my solidarity with the movement.

Pictures of Vietcong blown beyond recognition, or of innocent Vietnamese children, circulated through the dozens of new underground newspapers, which seemed to operate on the principle that it wasn't true if it wasn't obscene. Confusion reigned in the very institutions built to teach wisdom. In fact, the professors were often the ones telling us of American "imperialism," and that the plight of the Third World was actually the fault of the United States. It was America's greed, the product of capitalism, that should be on trial. We were urged to commit ourselves to the cause of North Vietnam—to become the "Americong." There was political rhetoric everywhere on campus, from the classroom to the lunchroom. Even the restroom graffiti took a leftist bent, away from the typical sexual themes.

What was the overall effect of all this? Was it raising the collective conscience of American youth, particularly those on the campuses? Although I had a few friends who were reading Karl Marx and Frantz Fanon, if you had asked the majority of us exactly what it was about Vietnam that we were protesting, we couldn't have told you. We just sensed that a war between generations was on and we'd better take sides. Each of us felt like the Omega Man, and that the destiny of the world hinged on who came out on top. Buffalo Springfield captured it well in their song "For What It's Worth":

There's something happening here.
What it is ain't exactly clear.
There's a man with a gun over there,
tellin' me I've got to beware. . . .

Paranoia strikes deep,
Into your life it will creep.
It starts when you're always afraid.
Step out of line the men come and take you away.

You better stop, hey, what's that sound?
Ev'rybody look what's goin down. . . .[8]

Racial and political unrest found its way into the music of folk-rock singers and onto the airwaves of America. Even the folk-rock group I was in began to write songs about the uncivil "civil war" that was ripping our country apart. A sampling of the lyrics from a handful of folk-rock artists of the era illustrates the mood of the times:

How many deaths will it take till he knows
That too many people have died?[9]

If I had a hammer. . .
I'd hammer out a warning . . . .
It's the hammer of justice,
It's the bell of freedom. . .
All over this land.[10]
We're on the eve of destruction.[11]

How many dead men will it take
To build a dike that will not break?
How many children must we kill
Before we make the waves stand still?[12]

These lyrics are obviously quite removed from the "lay off of my blue suede shoes" words of the previous decade!

The sixties was a decade of intensity. In less than five years, we had witnessed the assassinations of President Kennedy, Malcolm X, Martin Luther King, Jr., and Senator Robert Kennedy; the gradual erosion of the nonviolent sector of the black rights movement; the unleashing of militant demonstration and destruction as the supposed prerequisite to national peace; and the merger of the political Left and the "flower children" into what historians have collectively called "the counterculture."

If passions had been de-emphasized in the fifties, the decade that followed was ruled by feelings rather than facts. The stronger the commitment, the more "righteous" the action.

BETTER LIVING THROUGH CHEMISTRY?

The sixties contained a third and vital ingredient. If rock-and-roll was the state religion, and the political Left the high priests, then drugs could easily be labeled the sacrament of the sixties. Scholars have argued for years regarding which came first, the "rocker" or the "doper." The lyrical output and lifestyles of the rock stars certainly perpetuated and embellished the drug scene, but drugs were also a part of the beat culture, which had virtually nothing to do with rock.

Ideology pervaded and became the lasting legacy of drug use in the sixties In the sixties, drugs were an integral part of an entire "anti-establishment" worldview that was foisted upon us, and which many gladly accepted. Drug use was an ideology; it was not merely a behavioral phenomenon. The drug problem of the nineties is certainly the offspring of the sixties lifestyle, but that is where the similarity ends. There is no intellectual or personal quest behind drug use today. It is either escapist or hedonistic, not ideological.

This is not an attempt to evade the legitimate guilt and blame that should fall upon the sixties generation. It is simply an effort to clarify that, although pleasure was certainly one of the driving forces in drug use then, it was not the only force. Many honestly believed that drugs were a key vehicle in raising our nation's consciousness and hopefully awakening its conscience. A grand illusion, to be sure, but it was a genuine belief among many of those who smoked, dropped, and shot the drugs of the decade.

The following description of the motive behind one California "chemist" captures the ideological connection between drugs and the counterculture:

> Expert chemists like the Bay Area's Owsley, who set up underground laboratories and fabricated potent and pure LSD tablets in the hundreds of thousands, were not in it just for the money; they kept their prices down, gave out plenty of free samples, and fancied themselves dispensers of miracles at the service of a new age—"architects of social change" with a "mission . . . to change the world," in the words of one of Owsley's apprentices.[13]

Drugs were viewed as an aid to social change. Many users believed drugs brought insight into the nature of America's social and political hypocrisy, as well as hope for a new world. Paul McCartney summarized the ideology well in a statement to *Life* magazine in 1967: "After I took it [LSD], it opened my eyes. We only use one tenth of our brain. Just think what all we could accomplish if we could only tap that hidden part! It would mean a whole new world. If the politicians would take LSD, there wouldn't be any more war, or poverty or famine."[14]

The counterculture wanted politicians to take acid instead of bribes. It was that simple. But there was a serious flaw in the "better living through chemistry" approach to life. For some reason, it didn't last and couldn't be translated into pedestrian-level life on earth. I recall spending an entire evening wasted beyond belief on some opiated hashish, studying the surface of an orange! I honestly believed that I had discovered something that would benefit humanity. Of course, when morning came my revelation left.

Some of the heavy drug users on our campus who became Christians in the early seventies actually brought the drug ideology into their new faith. They planned to buy property in northern Wisconsin, raise dope, bring nonbelievers to their farm, and get them high so they would be more susceptible and open to the gospel! Ludicrous in hindsight, but a powerful testimony to just how deeply the belief in the redemptive power of drugs had permeated our generation.

Drug use was to be a mystical experience. "LSD is Western yoga," said Timothy Leary, the Harvard sociology-professor-turned-drug-guru. "The aim of all Eastern religion, like the aim of LSD, is basically to get high; that is, to expand your consciousness and find ecstasy and revelation within."[15] His partner in crime, Ken Kesey, said it even more poetically:

> The first drug trips were for most of us shell-shattering ordeals that left us blinking knee deep in the cracked crusts of our pie-in-the-sky personalities. Suddenly people were stripped before one another and behold: we were beautiful. Naked and helpless and sensitive as a snake after skinning but far more human than that shining nightmare that had stood creaking in previous parade rest. We were alive and life was with us.[16]

Kesey's fluent metaphors were typical of those who had broken over to the "other side" and come back with tales of marvel to tell and sell. The appeal of drugs was enhanced by Kesey and those like him who spoke the foreign language of hallucinogenic drugs. It served to create a sort of we/they phenomenon in which they possessed the wisdom and insight that we needed.

Much of the music of the decade also carried the call to "turn on." Jimi Hendrix sang about a "Purple Haze" in his brain that changed his perception of things. Steppenwolf's "Magic Carpet Ride" spoke about being taken places one could not normally go. The Beatles' "Lucy in the Sky with Diamonds" described a land unknown to hallucinogen virgins, speaking of a boat drifting down a river bordered by "tangerine trees" and enveloped in "marmalade skies." The Jefferson Airplane's hit "White Rabbit" talked of drug experiences in terms of allusions to the classic tale *Alice in Wonderland*.

Some songs explicitly promoted drugs and drug-taking; but there was also an abundance of musicians whose music was commonly accepted to be best appreciated when the listener was high. The Doors' name was inspired by Aldous Huxley's poem about mescaline, "Doors of Perception."[17] Moody Blues and the later Beatles also fit this category. When asked what type of lifestyle the Sgt. Pepper's album was portraying, former Beatle Paul McCartney said, "Drugs, basically. They got reflected in the music. . . . Remember, drug-taking in 1967 was much more in the musicians' tradition. We'd heard of Ellington and Basie and jazz guys smoking a bit of pot, and now it arrived on our music scene. It started to find its way into everything we did, really. It coloured our perceptions."[18]

Drugs were as ubiquitous as rock music, and usually as accessible. The Catholic priest on our campus was considered "cool" because he got high with the rest of us. We never felt the need to question his orientation, even when he allowed the Newman Center to be used for seminars on witchcraft (taught by one of the English professors). The taking of drugs somehow pre-empted the need for logic and consistency because "we" were living on a higher plane and consequently had a better view of reality than "they" had.

The sixties was a complex time, and understanding it in retrospect is difficult. But the threads that were loose and dangling as the fifties ended became tightly woven into a discernible lifestyle during the sixties. And as the sixties drew to a close, it appeared, if for only a moment, that wisdom actually did reside with the youth of America.

NOTES

1. Jim Miller, "The Beach Boys," *The Rolling Stone Illustrated History of Rock and Roll* (New York: Random, 1976), pp. 158, 160.
2. Ibid., p. 162.
3. "I Am My Words," *The Sixties* (New York: Newsweek, 1987), p. 29.
4. Paul Johnson, *Modern Times* (New York: Harper & Row, 1983), p. 633.
5. Dwight D. Eisenhower, *Public Papers* (1959), p. 71.
6. A fairly detailed account of these efforts is documented in the personal memoirs of former radical David Harris in his book *Dreams Die Hard* (New York: St. Martins/Marek, 1982).
7. *This Fabulous Century*, vol. 7 (Alexandria, Va.: Time-Life, 1970), p. 30.
8. "For What It's Worth," Stephen Stills, ©1966 Cotillion Music Inc., Ten East Music, and Springalo Toones. All rights on behalf of Cotillion Music Inc. administered by Warner-Tamerlane Publishing Corp. All rights reserved. Used by permission.
9. "Blowin' in the Wind," Bob Dylan, ©1962 Warner Bros. Inc. All rights reserved. Used by permission.
10. "If I Had a Hammer," words and music by Lee Hays and Pete Seeger, ©1958 (renewed) and 1962 (renewed) Ludlow Music, Inc., New York. Used by permission.
11. "Eve of Destruction," words and music by P. F. Sloan, ©1965 by MCA Music Publishing, a Division of MCA Inc., New York 10019. Used by permission. All rights reserved.
12. "Saigon Bride," by Nina Dusheck and Joan Baez. Copyright ©1967 Robbins Music Corporation. Rights Assigned to EMI Catalogue Partnership. All rights controlled and administered by EMI Robbins Catalog Inc. All rights reserved. International copyright secured. Used by permission.
13. Todd Gitlin, *The Sixties: Years of Hope, Days of Rage* (Toronto: Bantam, 1987), p. 214.
14. "The Beatles," *Life*, June 16, 1967, p. 105.
15. *This Fabulous Century*, vol. 7, p. 84.
16. Ken Kesey, quoted by Derek Taylor in *It Was Twenty Years Ago Today* (New York: Simon & Schuster, 1987), p. 98. Kesey and nineteen others took the ultimate trip by converting a bus into a caravan of madness, doing LSD on their "magic bus" as an experiment. Author Tom Wolfe documented the journey in his book *The Electric Kool-Aid Acid Test*. (New York: Bantam, 1983).
17. Gitlin, *The Sixties: Years of Hope*, p. 216.
18. Quoted by Taylor in *It Was Twenty Years Ago Today*, p. 88.

All political systems are on the way out. We're finally gonna get to the point where there's no more bigotry or greed or war. Peace is on the way. . . . People are simply gonna learn that they can get more by being groovy than by being greedy.

Arlo Guthrie
as quoted in
This Fabulous Century

Got no deeds to do, no promises to keep.
I'm dappled and drowsy and ready to sleep.
Let the morning-time drop all its petals on me.
Life, I love you, all is groovy.

Paul Simon
"59th Street Bridge Song"

4

ALL IS GROOVY

America shuddered as the sixties came to a close. *Time* magazine has called 1968 "the year [that] severed past from future."[1] The late sixties may have created a signpost in history, but the decade fractured countless relationships as well. Family life in America suffered more casualties than ever before. Annie Gottlieb's comments are chilling:

> If the right wing gets to write history, they will put us down not as the "Love Generation," but as the generation that destroyed the American family. They will point to the soaring rates of divorce, venereal disease, teen pregnancy, and abortion as sequelae of the Sixties. If they are right in their attribution of blame, then, ironically, the Sixties generation achieved one of our main objectives.
>
> We might not have been able to tear down the state, but the family was closer. We could get our hands on it. And, like the Confucian Chinese, we believed that the family was the foundation of the state, as well as the collective state of mind. To us, its children, the Fifties nuclear family—with its hypocrisies, its covert power struggles, its substitution of materialism for love—was the cornerstone of the Nuclear Age. We truly believed that the family had to be torn apart to free love, which alone could heal the damage done when the atom was split to release energy.

And the first step was to tear ourselves free from our parents.[2]

Parents, including my own, were accused of being shallow and dishonest. We demanded depth, honesty (often the sixties' excuse for disrespect and vulgarity), and transparency. In retrospect, it was comparable to expecting my father (who had been forced to drop out of high school to feed his family) to explain quantum mechanics to a college physics class. Our parents had been raised to work hard and play fair, not to introspect and emote. Sadly, for many, this inability to communicate made their own children seem like foreign exchange students.

But the family was not the only battleground. Indeed, it seemed that everyone was fighting. In 1968 the Tet Offensive pushed forward in Vietnam. And at the Democratic National Convention in Chicago, demonstrators captured the nation's sympathy by chanting, "The whole world is watching!" as Mayor Daley's police attacked them. In 1970, the Ohio National Guard fought campus protestors at Kent State, from which the picture of a girl screaming over the body of a dead student emerged as a permanent part of our collective psyche. But that psyche was subtly changing.

The counterculture was anything but a cohesive whole. Many whose minds are clouded with the fog of nostalgia, or who are simply students of the decade but were not participants, seem to think that all of us living then were of one mind and soul, that all of us were politically astute and militantly active. This is a faulty caricature. A few centers of rage easily and repeatedly captured the focus of the media: Berkeley for free speech; Oakland for the Black Panthers; San Francisco for Gay Pride; Chicago, Detroit, and Newark for race riots; and Columbia University for student takeovers, just to mention the more obvious ones. The young people captured by TV in all these places had an uncanny sameness. An understandable but faulty conclusion was that all American youth were as informed and impassioned about the causes of the sixties as the counterculture "stars" who appeared nightly on the news.

The political Left and the bulk of the counterculture popularly known as "hippies" were distant cousins at best. At the nucleus of the leftist viewpoint were people like Fay Stender, Huey Newton, Tom Hayden, and Abbie Hoffman. They were the "movers and shakers" who had the nation's eye or at least the camera's eye during the decade. They wrote the books, led the marches, and fought the law. But they were not symbols of the entire sixties generation, only part of it. Moving out from this nucleus of rage were varying degrees of *bona fide* commitment to the issues of the era. The misleading common denominator was the counterculture lifestyle (i.e., drugs, sex, and music) and the uniform (jeans, tee shirts, and long hair). We all shared the same dressing room, so to speak, but when we walked out we went in different directions.

Personally, I was politically illiterate, but I thought deeply about life. I shared the spirit of the leftists, but I didn't bolster my uneasiness with *Ramparts* magazine or Jerry Rubin. I was simply empty inside. Something was missing in my life. I wanted to talk about how I felt, and I discovered that a lot of kids my age did too. I even tried to bring my questions into my music. When the folk-rock group I was in did warm-up for B. J. Thomas in Saint Paul, his repertoire included songs like "Raindrops" while we were singing songs about the war.

I didn't study Marx, Che Guevara, or Chairman Mao, but I did do drugs, listen to the music of the era, and protest the war. My allegiance, however, was not with the political Left—it was with my friends. And my interest was not primarily to see an improved America but to fill a growing void within myself. In an effort to belong, I simply wanted to be doing what everyone else was doing. That's a shallow commitment to changing the world, but it was my "orbit," as well as that for most youth in the sixties.

I think that many of us who lived through the sixties era suffer from a sort of countercultural amnesia when it comes to either the degree or motivation of our involvement in the movement. It's similar to old anglers recalling the size of the fish they caught when they were young. Grateful Dead leader Jerry Garcia, in a recent *Rolling Stone* interview, admitted, "For me, the lame part of the sixties was the political part, the social part. The real part was the spiritual part."[3]

The "spiritual part" Garcia speaks of was the search, the quest for some meaning to life apart from accumulating goods. Most of the sixties generation shared that passion. And in the minds of a growing majority, meaning was to be found through experience. The austere image of the leftist radical was much less appealing than the pleasure-seeking lifestyle of the flower child. In short, for most of us, partying was preferable to politics. Though many radicals and cultural revolutionaries searched for a "convergence, trying to nudge the New Left and the counterculture together,"[4] most American youth thought the war had degenerated from a reality to a cause, moving further and further from their own world on its way to the nether world of statistics and rhetoric. Protesting the war had deteriorated from a passion to an occupation.

A friend of mine was attending Berkeley in the sixties, and his commentary on what went on was revealing. Apparently, he had to drive past the California Highway Patrol post in Oakland every morning on his way to class. He saw the patrol file out of the station like clockwork every day at 8:00 A.M. By the time they reached the Berkeley campus, the demonstrators were beginning to arrive. And almost as if on cue, the TV trucks would pull up at the same time. The protesters protested, the police policed, and the TV reporters reported. They all did their job until 5:00 P.M. when the TV crews went home to their wives and children. Then, a reverse migration occurred after the television trucks left. First the protestors would trickle off, followed by the highway patrol. This daily routine was as predictable as an episode of a soap opera.

This phenomenon of the spontaneous-become-routine had a detrimental effect. It diminished the sense of passion and belonging for those on the edges of commitment. People simply do not maintain involvement in issues that are impersonal, vague, or distant. Trying to topple the system or protest a war on the other side of the world seemed noble, but eventually lacked the intimate personal contact needed to perpetuate commitment and involvement. For those of us on the fringes, the movement lost its motion.

This growing apathy even affected the reaction to the assassinations of Martin Luther King, Jr., and Bobby Kennedy in 1968. Youthful idealism staggered under the distinct possibility that even if you do get to a position where you can help others, you may be killed. The rhetorical question, "What's the use?" reared its ugly head. For our parents, there seemed to be a pause in the pandemonium. And they could point to the landing of the Apollo 11 spacecraft on the moon in July of 1969 as evidence that America was moving forward and that, despite the noise and clamor of the decade, things were starting to look like home again.

The disruptions on the campuses, though still intense, were diminishing in number, and the majority of American youth seemed to be adopting the hippie lifestyle rather than the austere activist motif. This pleased the parent culture because, although bizarre and equally unconventional, hippies were not as violent as their leftist brothers. On the surface, things seemed to be returning to normal.

For the adolescent masses, things looked the best ever. The United States was preparing to begin withdrawals from Vietnam. The flower children, whose flag was the peace symbol and whose state flower was cannabis, seemed to be usurping the public eye. Moral "uptightness" seemed to be weakening as living together and homosexuality began to be recognized as valid alternative lifestyles. A sense of solidarity filled the hearts of the counterculture youth. Suddenly, it seemed as though we were a *bona fide* counterculture, not merely some anomaly. In the words of Janis Joplin, "There's lots and lots of us, more than anybody ever thought before. We used to think of ourselves as little clumps of weirdos. But now we're a whole new minority group."[5] The counterculture became (and remains) the object of serious study by sociologists. As members of the movement, we were beginning to believe that all the riots, sit-ins, marches, and speeches had actually accomplished something of substantial value and lasting worth. Although we had only participated in spirit, even those of us on the fringes wanted to share the spoils of victory. We honestly believed we had hard evidence of our success. In January 1967, San Francisco's Golden Gate Park was the receptacle into which nearly ten thousand "long hairs" poured themselves for the first "Human Be-In." In their February 6, 1967, issue, *Newsweek* gave this account:

> They wore blowsy furs, fresh flowers, jangling beads, floppy-brimmed hats, even Indian war paint. They waved sticks of burning incense, swirled abstractly designed banners, tooted on fifes and recorders. There under the warm sun with the faithful was the whole range of the hippie hierarchy. Poet Allen Ginsberg tried to lead the crowd in a Hare Krishna swami chant; Timothy Leary, headmaster of the LSD school, delivered a plea to "turn on, tune in and drop out," and Pig-Pen, the pop organist whose gaudy sweatshirts have become standard apparel for hundreds of teen-age girls, invoked the hippies via another favorite idiom—rock music.[6]

The Human Be-In was a caricature of what the counterculture itself had become—an altruistic stew of nonpolitical politics, naive idealism, Eastern mysticism, drugs, sex, and rock-and-roll. On October 21, 1967, a large gathering even made a seemingly serious attempt to exorcize the demons of war and death by "levitating" the Pentagon! 1967 also saw the "Summer of Love" in San Francisco. In the words of Todd Gitlin: "Only fifty or seventy-five thousand young pilgrims poured into the Haight-Ashbury for the Summer of Love, but they were at the center of the nation's fantasy life. Music, dress, language, sex, and intoxicant habits changed with breathtaking speed."[7]

If what happened in Golden Gate Park and Haight-Ashbury was seen as tangible evidence of the reality and per-
manence of the counterculture, then what would occur two
years later on the other side of the continent would prove beyond any doubt that a new age was about to dawn. In August
1969, four hundred thousand card-carrying members of the
counterculture converged on a dairy farm owned by Max
Yasgur in Bethel, New York, for what was billed as the Woodstock Music and Art Fair: An Aquarian Exposition, known
forever after simply as Woodstock.

Today, just say the word and people have flashes of nostalgia. Most members of the baby boom generation know
about Woodstock. It was perceived as a countercultural
event of the grandest magnitude. The optimism responsible
for its inflated importance was almost universal among the
counterculture near the close of the decade. And as always,
this optimism was reflected clearly in our music:

> If you're going to San Francisco,
> Be sure to wear some flowers in your hair.
> If you're going to San Francisco,
> You're gonna meet some gentle people there. . . .
>
> All across the nation, such a strong vibration. . . .
> There's a whole generation with a new explanation.[8]

A summary statement on the countercultural mood at the
decade's end is the theme song from the rock musical *Hair*,
made popular by the pop group The 5th Dimension. Consider these familiar lyrics in their proper historical-cultural
context:

> When the moon is in the seventh house,
> And Jupiter aligns with Mars,
> Then peace will guide the planets
> And love will steer the stars;
> This is the dawning of the age of Aquarius, . . .
> Harmony and understanding, sympathy and trust abounding.

No more falsehoods or derisions,
Golden living dreams of visions,
Mystic crystal revelation, and the mind's true liberation.[9]

We believed that a new age was dawning—the fruit of all the love we had generated. We honestly anticipated that after the smoke cleared, the country would see clearly that we knew what we were talking about. The counterculture would become the accepted culture. We believed that we were the true architects of the Great Society. Our children and grandchildren would be the beneficiaries of our blood, sweat, and tears. We would be heroes!

Although it is true that our children did inherit the fruit of our labors (as we shall see in the next section), we never could have dreamed what a foul harvest it would be.

The decade that almost destroyed a nation was coming to a close, and the nation's youth held their breath and waited. We were going back to the best of times once more! But, if disillusion is the child of illusion, then despair is its grandchild. The darkest days were just ahead.

Notes

1. Lance Morrow, "1968," *Time* (January 11, 1988), p. 16.
2. Annie Gottlieb, *Do You Believe in Magic?* (New York: Time, 1987), pp. 234-35.
3. "The Rolling Stone Interview," *Rolling Stone* (November 30, 1989), p. 73.
4. Quoted in *The Sixties* (New York: Newsweek, 1987), p. 23.
5. Todd Gitlin, *The Sixties: Years of Hope, Days of Rage* (Toronto: Bantam, 1987), p. 213.
6. *The Sixties* (New York: Newsweek, 1987), p. 22.
7. Todd Gitlin, *The Sixties: Years of Hope*, p. 215.
8. "San Francisco (Be Sure to Wear Some Flowers in Your Hair)," words and music by John Phillips, 1967 by MCA Music Publishing, a Division of MCA Inc., New York 10019. Used by permission. All rights reserved.
9. "Aquarius, Let the Sunshine In," by Gerome Ragni and James Rado. Copyright ©1966, 1967, 1968, 1970; James Rado, Gerome Ragni, Galt MacDermot, Nat Shapiro, United Artists Music Co., Inc. All rights controlled by United Artists Music Co., Inc. All rights of United Artists Music Co., Inc. assigned to EMI Catalogue Partnership. All rights administered by EMI UNART Catalog Inc. International copyright secured. Made in USA. All rights reserved.

People try to put us down
Just because we get around.
Things they do look awful cold.
Hope I die before I get old . . .
Talkin' 'bout my generation.

Pete Townshend
"My Generation"

While he was still speaking, yet another messenger came
and said, "Your sons and daughters were feasting and
drinking wine at the oldest brother's house, when suddenly
a mighty wind swept in from the desert and struck the four
corners of the house. It collapsed on them and they are
dead."

Job 1:18-19

5

ALL JOB'S CHILDREN

Almost before our eyes the Aquarian Dream turned into a nightmare. We were like modern-day children of Job; the roof of our house caved in on us while we were at the climax of our party. The radiant optimism of the latter sixties turned into a dark pessimism by the time the seventies were underway. A mournful cry of the soul permeated the youth culture. These lyrics were written during the opening years of the new decade by the same artists who were singing the glowing songs of hope only a few years earlier:

> You used to say live and let live. . . .
> But if this ever-changing world in which we live in
> Makes you give it a cry,
> Say live and let die.[1]

> Ashes to ashes, dust to dust,
> We'll never be the same.
> We're all forgiven
> Because we're only livin'
> To leave the way we came.[2]

If Woodstock, in August 1969, had been perceived as the undeniable proof of the solidarity and wisdom of the counterculture, then Altamont, a San Francisco area concert in December of the same year, would show evidence that the counterculture was falling apart:

> At the end of their 1969 U.S. tour, the Rolling Stones planned a free concert near San Francisco. It came to be called a festival, and despite the fact that the site was changed less than 24 hours before the show, some 300,000 fans converged on the Altamont Speedway, near a freeway about 40 miles southeast of San Francisco. There was no way that basic necessities could be provided for so many people on such short notice, and Altamont turned into a nightmare of drug casualties, stench from toilets and fires and food and vomit, faulty sound, and finally, the brutal violence visited on the audience by pool cue- and knife-wielding Hell's Angels who said they had been hired (by the Stones and cosponsors Grateful Dead, for $500 worth of beer) as security guards. The climax came as the Stones played late in the day, when a young black man drew a gun, and was knifed repeatedly by Angels; he died, as three others had in the course of the day. (There had been deaths at Woodstock, but they had been conveniently overlooked in all the romantic youth-cult hype.) Altamont was hailed as the end of the counterculture; more accurately, it was a graphic symbol for what the counterculture had in truth become.[3]

The year 1970 witnessed the drug-related deaths of Jimi Hendrix, Janis Joplin, and the Doors' Jim Morrison, as well as the intensely emotional and spiteful breakup of the Beatles. Change came to my own life as well. Our folk-rock group disbanded. A sociology professor who had preached morally relativistic lifestyles was found dead in her car in the garage—the engine running. Another Marxist sociology professor, who had called the apostle Paul a bastard and was the leader of a commune, lost all of the commune's funds in a pool game at a local bar. My philosophy professor, who had exploited his academic freedom by having his students chant four-letter words at the top of our lungs until our "moral hang-ups" about those words evaporated, was fired for sexual misconduct with coeds.

I spent that summer living in Minneapolis in an area known as the West Bank, a sort of miniature Haight-Ashbury in the Midwest. I watched hippie "brothers" steal each others' drugs, money, and bedmates. It slowly became evident that the solidarity I thought I was part of was a sham.

My wife's counterculture group began to unravel before her eyes as well. She started to seriously question the validity and integrity of the movement when friends sat and laughed at one of their brothers as he burned his arms with lit cigarettes while high on speed. Others in her world ended up in institutions because of drugs or mental problems. She watched as one layer after another of the veneer of authenticity slowly eroded from her ideology.

What had happened? How do you explain the overwhelming evidence that an entire generation appeared to be chronically depressed? Was it merely a cultural hangover after an enormous national party, or was it symptomatic of something much deeper? Annie Gottlieb captures succinctly the tell tale truth of what had happened:

> Like all reactions, the Anti-America drew its energy from that which it opposed. When the war ended and Nixon resigned, its necessary destructive work was finished and its energy ebbed. Constructive work would take much longer, and it could not be achieved by the mere amassing of bodies. "No" can be shouted from a million throats, "yes" is said face-to-face in response to love or reason. . . . The counterculture was only a negative. We just said "no" to whatever the Old America had said "yes" to.[4]

What Gottlieb says about the Left applies to the entire sixties youth culture. It was simply a reaction, a cultural knee-jerk response to what was wrong with America. We were critics of the present social order, with no sense of responsibility, much less a plan, for the new order we were clamoring for.

Tearing America down had been easy. Rebuilding had never crossed our minds. Former radical Peter Collier, writ-

ing to a friend who had accused him of abandoning the leftist cause, maintains that the heart of the political Left had
nothing to do with construction, only demolition:

> Take a careful look at what you still believe, because it is a
> mirror of the dark center of the radical heart: not compassion
> but resentment—the envious whine of have not and want; not
> the longing for justice but the desire for revenge; not a quest
> for peace but a call to arms. It is war that feeds the true radi-
> cal passions, which are not altruism and love but nihilism
> and hate.[5]

The thought that we had any responsibility for, much
less complicity in, the evils of this system had never entered
our minds. But by the end of the decade, it began to dawn on
us that we had shouted "murder" only to discover blood on
our own hands. We were a part of the problem because we
were not part of the solution.

This ambiguous relationship of the counterculture with
"imperialistic Amerika" is perhaps best exemplified by the
industry that fueled the sixties rebellion in the first place—
rock music. The Rolling Stones are an excellent example of
our ability to live with paradox. It was easy for Mick Jagger
to sing about being a poor boy who had to sing for a living.[6]
He preached against money, yet his family had money, and
so did he. Life was very comfortable politically, and conveniently profitable professionally. Stuart Goldman uncovers
the true politics beneath this obvious contradiction:

> So, if rock is neither conservative nor Marxist nor liberal, that
> leaves the anti-authority doctrine of anarchism. This is
> nearer to the mark; rockers routinely denounce "the system"
> —governments, parents, teachers, etc. However, they usually
> do this while driving around in limos, talking on car phones
> with managers, lawyers, and accountants. Ask any young rock-
> er his dream and you'll find that it involves wealth, fame, and
> power.
>
> Rock politics, in short, is a sort of parasitic anarchism.
> Rockers are comfortably aware that the hated system will

doubtless outlive them, continuing to provide its despised benefits. At the heavy-metal extreme, this becomes a form of hypocritical nihilism in which all the normal values of civilized decency are sneered at and—in everyday business transactions—relied upon.[7]

Rock activists continue to play on both teams. The "We Are the World" phenomenon gave the world the message that rockers are deeply compassionate and giving people, subtly turning our gaze away from their day-to-day eccentric and hedonistic lifestyle. Taking a few bucks out of your front pocket to give to charity is one way to encourage people to put money in your back pocket!

We who identified with the sixties counterculture were parasitic anarchists to be sure. And when nearly every institution in the land wilted under the shouting masses, we had to face the fact that, in a sort of surrealistic twist of events, we were now in the driver's seat. It was much like the sniveling, whining neighbor boy who always wanted to be quarterback suddenly being given the ball and asked what the next play is. It's easy being a parasite until your host organism dies!

When we pulled down the walls of authority, the boundaries that provided some sense of meaning to society, we had no alternative to put in its place. We hadn't considered that we would need a "countersystem." This naive ignorance of the complexities of society was part of our youthful idealism. But as the smoke of the era cleared, it became more and more apparent that we were guilty of more than mere rebellion.

Much of the motivation for our actions was blatantly selfish. The movement with its causes became a justifiable excuse for most of us to throw off the restraints of the previous decade with a certain warped sense of mission and dignity, and to absorb ourselves in personal pleasures. One of the most sobering testimonies to this truth is contained within the pages of Bob Greene's book, *Homecoming*.[8] It contains letter after letter from Vietnam vets who were spit upon, cursed, and made targets for flying garbage and soiled diapers. The harsh reality may be that the "peace movement" was not committed to peace, only some vague idea of peace. Or even perhaps worse, that some of the anti-war sentiment may have been simply a fear of being drafted.

We were passionately driven by causes but were somehow deaf to accusations of irresponsibility. This is still true today. If you read most of the memoirs of former sixties radicals, you will find nothing even remotely resembling remorse. Former radical Tom Hayden, in his autobiography, *Reunion*, boasts: "We of the sixties accomplished more than most generations in American history."[9] Hayden's statement is true. But one could just as easily say that the bomb dropped on Hiroshima "accomplished" more than any bomb in history.

The counterculture of the sixties had played catch with a nation. But by the decade's end that nation lay shattered like a piece of mishandled china. With the unguarded honesty that permeates their recollection of the decade, Peter Collier and David Horowitz admit:

> The Sixties might have been a time of tantalizing glimpses of the New Jerusalem. But it was also a time when the "System"—that collection of values that provide guidelines for societies as well as individuals—was assaulted and mauled. As one center of authority after another was discredited under the New Left offensive, we radicals claimed that we murdered to create. But while we wanted a revolution, we didn't have a plan. The decade ended with a big bang that made society into a collection of splinter groups, special interest organizations and newly minted "minorities," whose only common belief was that America was guilty and untrustworthy. This is perhaps the enduring legacy of the Sixties.[10]

I have migrated from uneasiness, to disgust, to anger over the edited and romanticized versions of our era, written and propagated by those who feel no responsibility to try to clean up the debris from our "party." The present generation has inherited the miscarriage of the Aquarian Dream—a dismal moral and spiritual environment in which to grow. And I'm disgusted with my own generation's refusal to admit our responsibility for that environment or to face up to the pivotal role they will play in the future stability of our nation.

We of the sixties need to recognize the consequences of our past actions. For they have created the conditions that have put the present generation—and our nation—at risk. The collapse of the sixties' social agenda created a new watershed out of which three main streams flowed—three avenues of attempted emotional and intellectual exit from the decade of illusion: irrational optimism, hedonism, and mysticism. Those three streams have grown into raging torrents into which today's youth are rafting without caution.

NOTES

1. "Live and Let Die," by Paul and Linda McCartney, Copyright ©1973. United Artists Music Co,. Ltd. and MPL Communications, Inc. Rights for United Artists Music Co., Assigned to EMI Catalogue Partnership and controlled and administered by EMI UNART Catalog Inc. All rights reserved. International copyright secured. Used by permission.

2. "Ashes to Ashes," words and music by Dennis Lambert and Brian Potter, ©1972 by Duchess Music Corporation. Rights administered by MCA Music Publishing, a Division of MCA Inc., New York 10019. Used by permission. All rights reserved.

3. John Morthland, "Rock Festivals," *The Rolling Stone Illustrated History of Rock and Roll* (New York: Random, 1976), pp. 308, 310.

4. Annie Gottlieb, *Do You Believe in Magic?* (New York: Time, 1987), pp. 75-76.

5. Peter Collier and David Horowitz, *Destructive Generation: Second Thoughts About the Sixties* (New York: Summit, 1989), p. 306.

6. See "Street Fighting Man," words and music by Mick Jagger and Keith Richard (Abkco Music, 1968).

7. Stuart Goldman, "That Old Devil Music," *National Review*, February 24, 1989, 31.

8. Bob Greene, *Homecoming: When the Soldiers Returned from Vietnam* (New York: G. P. Putnam's Sons, 1989).

9. Quoted by Collier and Horowitz, *Destructive Generation*, p. 240.

10. Collier and Horowitz, *Destructive Generation*, p. 15.

We ended a war, toppled two presidents, desegregated the South, broke other barriers of discrimination. How could we accomplish so much and have so little in the end?

Tom Hayden
as quoted in *Newsweek*,
September 5, 1988

6

HAPPY DAYS ARE HERE AGAIN

Recently, my wife and I struck up a conversation with a teenaged clerk in a local department store. I had just purchased a book about the sixties and while we were checking out, she commented, "Oh, I wish I had lived during the sixties." When we queried her as to why, she responded, "Back then you guys believed in something. I want to believe in something."

The current attempt of so many of her contemporaries to embrace the memorabilia-become-relics of the sixties, the "peace" symbol, tie-dye clothing, and the incredible popularity of sixties' music all point to an infatuation with the popularized history of the sixties. And while many of these young people may look to that era out of a desire for personal meaning, their perspective on the sixties is limited. They see it as a time of intense passions and commitment. They know nothing of its enormous failure, the fruit of which was largely responsible for the very emptiness they are experiencing.

When I was a senior in college, campus radicals were evaporating like the morning mist. It seemed as though everybody we knew either had bailed out themselves or at least had seen their friends leave college, disenchanted and lost. The casualties were numerous. Bad drug trips, unexpected pregnancies, broken relationships, and even death colored our generation's political and social résumé.

Gradually we realized that it is not enough merely to demand answers of others. True skepticism also demands scrutiny of itself. To be intellectually honest, we should have asked penetrating questions of ourselves and our movement as well. But we hadn't. The decade of illusion was over, and a sense of emptiness ensued, as we realized that the movement had struck a dead end. Collier and Horowitz describe this emptiness: "By the early Seventies, a subtle panic had overtaken the Movement. The revolution that we had awaited so breathlessly was nearing the end of what we now realized would be a dry labor. The monstrous offspring of our fantasies would never be born."[1]

There was a genuine realization that the desired outcome of the movement had turned out to be a fantasy of overwhelming proportions. A popular poster during the decade had been, "What if they gave a war and no one came?" The countercultural equivalent became, "What if we promised a new era and it never appeared?" The rebels without a cause had perpetrated a cause without a hope.

Some of the sixties generation have recently accused the seventies kids of "dropping the ball" in regard to the movement they supposedly started. It would be more accurate to say that many of those directly involved simply wandered away from the movement in an attempt to deal with their own sense of disappointment, failure, and pain.

There were three basic responses to the collapse of the counterculture agenda of the sixties. The "road out of Dodge" forked into three discernible highways: irrational optimism, hedonism, and mysticism.

Counterculture Amnesia

We will look first at the irrational optimism response. The sixties' generation prided itself on its intellectual depth. But when lasting answers to the era's questions couldn't be found, some chose to abandon the use of reason. Basically they said, "We asked a lot of heavy questions in the sixties and didn't come up with any answers, so . . . let's pretend we never asked the questions!"

It is no coincidence that in the early seventies there appeared a short-lived but visible attempt to go back to a time when there were fewer problems—the fifties. Television shows like "Happy Days" and "LaVerne and Shirley," sitcoms built around the fifties' lifestyle, were suddenly popular.[2] In 1976, "Happy Days" was the number one program in all of television. In the words of TV historiographer Tim Brooks, "Nostalgia for the 1950s became big business in the mid-1970s."[3] In marking off eras of broadcasting history, Brooks calls the late 1960s to 1975 "The Relevance Era," and 1975-1980 "The ABC 'Fantasy' Era."[4] In other words, a distinct shift from the thoughtful to the thoughtless was evident in prime-time programming. Young adults wanted to forget the pain and frustration associated with the nagging, unanswered questions of the sixties.

Some of the music of the era reflected this abandonment of reason as well. John Denver's 1975 hit "Thank God I'm a Country Boy" talked of living in rural simplicity, where life was "nothin' but a funny, funny riddle."[5] His themes had no ideological connection to the music of the sixties. As music critic Janet Maslin described Denver: "Confessional, direct, projecting unremitting sincerity, Denver is ultimately more unfathomable than all the others put together. And his is such a complete, consistent, impenetrable persona that it discourages any efforts at understanding; he's so earnestly human that he lacks any air of humanity."[6]

Another example of this flight from intellectual themes was the popular brother/sister team, the Carpenters, with memorable but not particularly deep lyrics like "rainy days and Mondays always get me down." Classical rock-and-roll-style bands like Sha-Na-Na, Ten Years After, and Flash Cadillac and the Continental Kids suddenly found themselves back in style. There was a serious attempt by some artists to simply anesthetize the youth and make America feel good again. But to do so, or to seek to do so, was a denial of everything their peers had supposedly stood for in the previous decade.

RETURN OF THE DANCE

The disco phenomenon was another anemic attempt to forget the failure of the sixties. Polyester and jewelry replaced denim and suede. Although in reality it amounted to nothing more than a social puff on the youthscape, its brief appearance was significant. Disco was the first serious wholesale attempt within our nation's youth to return to a fifties fixture totally abandoned in the sixties—dancing.

As a musician myself during the sixties and early seventies, the demise of social dancing was very noticeable. All through high school, the rock band I was bassist for had played exclusively for dances. We performed at high schools, youth centers, bars, and even in church basements. But our services were always secured for the same reason, to provide music for young people to dance to. When I entered college in 1968, our campus still had a few dances, and a popular local bar featured live entertainment and a solid wood dance floor. But by the early seventies, the group I performed with only did "concerts"—a sort of musical Mexican standoff where the audience and performer faced each other all evening. Although the audience showed their enjoyment of what we did, they were essentially only passive spectators.

This concert mentality dominated the later years of the sixties and the early seventies. Nobody went to "dance to a band," they went to "hear a group." Music was designed and promoted to be experienced, rather than merely enjoyed. Dancing became counterproductive, even opposed, to the new intent of music.

The sudden appearance of disco in the seventies among the larger white youth culture was an abrupt deviation from what had become the norm in the sixties. It represented another attempt on the part of some to return to an era of fun rather than philosophy. *Newsweek* describes the music's appeal this way:

> The disco sound—that pounding music of minimum melody and a beefed-up beat—may be here to stay. What started a few years ago as all-night dance music in black and gay clubs has moved into the American heartland and is fast taking over the pop music business. Disco acts like those of Donna Summer and the Village People still rule the roost, but such pop stars as Dolly Parton and Barry Manilow are jumping into the disco pool—pushed by the public urge to dance, dance, dance.[7]

The desire to forget the sixties' failure was buoyed by disco even if the dance phenomenon was not a deliberate attempt by its originators to deal with the previous decade. But some in the music industry really wanted to make a clear statement about forgetting the heavy issues of the sixties. This anti-intellectual, "shallow-is-better" mentality is obvious in the Eagles' 1973 hit "Take It Easy."[8] According to this song, understanding was not as important as living freely. This was the pedestrian version of ivory-tower existentialism. Being was more important than knowing. But there were some in the music world who took the Eagles' advice a step further to the extreme of nihilism: being was not important either.

It was at this point in rock history that "punk rock" emerged. Fueled by high unemployment and the hypocrisy of wealthy British rockers like the Stones, a small group of musicians in England began to write and sing about the utter absurdity and emptiness of life. The Sex Pistols, the Damned, and the Clash were early punkers, making their debuts in the early seventies. Their attire included safety pins and paper clips through facial skin, copious swastikas, and a high dose of irreverence for anything held sacred. Punk rock was the music of irrationalism gone to seed—it was the music of anarchy. Its unfortunate progeny is with us today in the philosophy of neo-Nazi groups like the skinheads and in the lifestyle of many in the skateboard crowd.

RETURN OF THE DOLLAR

The seventies retreat to irrational optimism brought with it a renewed emphasis on material well-being. The condemnation of American materialism so characteristic of the sixties had been replaced, by the early eighties, by a growing consensus among young people that prosperity was a desirable life goal.

Consider, for example, a comparison of the results of a survey of 280,000 college freshmen conducted by the American Council on Education in two distinct periods.[9] Given the statement "A very important goal is to be well-off financially, 44 percent agreed in 1967; 69 percent agreed in 1982. In 1967, 83 percent of freshmen responding agreed "A very important goal is to develop a meaningful philosophy of life"; in 1982 only 47 percent of freshmen agreed. In 1967, 51 percent agreed "it is important to keep up with politics"; in 1982 the number agreeing dwindled to 38 percent.

The two survey dates are important. In 1967 the first baby boomers were twenty-one years old; in 1982 the last of the boomers entered college. Therefore, the data represent both those in the first wave of what became the counterculture and those at the end of the boomer generation. The differences in their ideological orientation are striking. When the sixties generation was at its apex, having an answer to the reason for one's existence was very important. But by the end of the 1970s, a total shift in values and ideology had occurred. The survey confirms college freshmen now considered making money more important than knowing why one was alive, and looking out for oneself was more important than looking out for others.

The collapse of the sixties' agenda caused youth and the aging baby boomers to retreat into an illusion of happy days and a life free of deep questions. But the sixties generation took a second "road out of Dodge," a highway to hedonism, that would have an even more devastating effect on the fiber of American society.

NOTES

1. Peter Collier and David Horowitz, *Destructive Generation: Second Thoughts About the Sixties* (New York: Summit, 1989), p. 268.

2. "Happy Days" began in January 1974 and aired for more than ten years. Its spin-off, "LaVerne and Shirley," first aired in January 1976. It was the number one program on TV in 1976. The theme song, "Making Our Dreams Come True," was in the top forty in 1976.

3. Tim Brooks and Earle Marsh, *The Complete Directory to Prime Time Network TV Shows 1946-Present* (New York: Ballentine, 1985), p. 323.

4. Ibid., pp. xvii-xviii.

5. John Sommers, "Thank God, I'm a Country Boy," Cherry Lane Music Co., 1975.

6. Janet Maslin, "Singer Songwriters," *The Rolling Stone Illustrated History of Rock and Roll* (New York: Random, 1976), pp. 318-19.

7. "The Disco Take-Over," *The Seventies* (New York: Newsweek, 1987), p. 28.

8. See "Take It Easy," words and music by Jackson Browne and Glen Fury (Swallow Turn Music, 1973).

9. Cheryl Russell, *100 Predictions for the Baby Boom* (New York: Plenum, 1987), pp. 43-44.

There is always one escape: into wickedness. Always do the thing that will shock and wound people. . . . Throw a little boy off a bridge, strike an old doctor across the face with a whip and break his spectacles—or, at any rate, dream about doing such things. . . . Gouge the eyes out of dead donkeys with a pair of scissors. Along those lines you can always feel yourself original. And after all, it pays!

George Orwell
"Benefit of Clergy"

7

ESCAPE INTO WICKEDNESS

A second response to the failure of the sixties' counterculture to provide an alternative to the despised and demo-
lished system was to *admit* that we had asked the questions
but *deny* that there were any lasting answers. The seventies'
version of Solomon's "Vanity, vanity, all is vanity" was "We
asked the heavy questions and we didn't get any heavy answers because there aren't any! Let's party 'til our eyes bleed!"
With the fervor of a Dionysian mob, many of the sixties generation took the freedoms they had won to new extremes.

Hedonism, the philosophy that pleasure is the highest
good, became a second road out of Dodge for many of the sixties' casualties. This visible preoccupation with pleasure was
particularly exploited in the area of sex. The counterculture
had rebelled against the sexual restraints and social mores
of the parent generation in the sixties, but illicit sexual behavior "went public" in the seventies. Sex in all its versions
and perversions was turned loose with a sense of earned dignity. Casual sex may have been a national pastime among
youth in the sixties, but it approached the status of an industry in the seventies, particularly within the rock music world.[1]

A no-holds-barred approach to sexual expression was a
predominant theme in much of the rock music of the seven-

ties. Mick Jagger may have rattled a few peoples' sensibilities in 1965 with his song "Satisfaction," but the Stones' albums in the early seventies, *Sticky Fingers* and *Hot Rocks*, left little to the imagination. (The *Sticky Fingers* album jacket featured a functional zipper on the crotch of a pair of skin-tight blue jeans.) Another group of the same era, Black Oak Arkansas, had an album titled *X-Rated*, which contained the songs "Bump and Grind," "Flesh Needs Flesh," and "Too Hot to Stop."

The theme of sex without limits degenerated even further to sex without civility. The glamour-rock band Kiss appeared in the early seventies singing to thirteen- to fifteen-year-olds about sex and sadomasochistic love in songs like "Sweet Pain." Their album *Love Gun* featured a song, "Plaster Caster," about a young female follower of rock musicians who made plaster casts of their genitals.[2] Elton John released "All the Girls Love Alice," about a lesbian, and "Sweet Painted Lady," touting the virtues of prostitution, in 1973. Soon the charts were peppered with songs by and about gay, lesbian, and transvestite musicians hawking their wares and worldview.

Although the vile nature of much contemporary music is obvious, we must seek to understand the context out of which that music emerged. It was not just the result of a few perverted musicians. The music of the seventies and its current offspring were one of the tragic consequences of the failure of the sixties' social agenda. The ludicrous and mindless antics of Alice Cooper and those like him would have been booed off the stage had they tried to tantalize the youth of the early and middle sixties. Yet by decade's end he had gained widespread acceptance. Between 1969 and 1976, eight of his albums passed the half-million sales mark. Senseless sex, the macabre, and sadomasochism, although not part of the counterculture ideology, unfortunately became part of its legacy in the seventies.

Many of us in today's adult generation who throw stones at the present youth culture and its music need to take a long and honest look in the mirror. The shallow excuse to our children that "our music was never as bad as yours" fails to account for the very real connection between the sixties and the eighties. Their music's ancestry is probably in a box in our garage!

Rambo Rock

Another expression of hedonism as sensual feeling during the early seventies appeared in rock music's violent themes. It was a natural carryover from the increased violence in the streets. The early experimenters and accepted founders of on-stage rock violence, The Who, popularized the theme of destruction with their concert finale of actually destroying their instruments. Slowly, destruction and death became legitimate rock themes.

In the early seventies, Alice Cooper performed the song "Dead Babies," from his *Killer* album, as he systematically chopped a doll to pieces on stage, flinging the fragments to screaming fans. This act concluded with a mock hanging of Cooper himself. The destructive motif carried over to the sexual as well, giving rise to one of the dominant themes of "heavy metal" rock: sadomasochism. Today, heavy metal groups Slayer, Metallica, and a host of others continue to churn out songs about suicide, sex, and destruction.[3]

The trivialization of evil is one of the most serious and least discussed effects of hedonism gone to seed. It affects all of us, not just the stoners and dopers who hang around the local convenience store. The continual pursuit of personal pleasure eventually produces a moral numbness—a desensitization to the finality and pain of death and the meaning of life. Consider this statement by social critic Stuart Goldman:

> It is music selling itself under the monicker of heavy metal, performed by groups like Slayer, Coven, the Damned, and Cycle Sluts From Hell, in which sex appears in its most blatant and perverse forms. Primarily pushing sadomasochistic sex, heavy metal does not neglect occultism, suicide, and murder.

You needn't go to a slasher film to see a woman being disemboweled in a satanic ritual—just turn on your local music video station. In short, rock has trivialized evil. Thus, songs like Slayer's "Spill the Blood" and "Mandatory Suicide," or the Misfit's "Can I Go Out and Kill Tonight?" are treated as silly or cute by the rock critics.[4]

Even Nintendo video games contribute to this trivialization of evil, violence, and pain. Children find it entertaining that they can maim and murder video versions of other human beings in the privacy of their rooms. Violence is quickly becoming a tolerated relational style for the rising generation.[5] This is becoming especially evident in the noticeable rise in playground violence among early elementary children. Schools are beginning to teach children "playground management" skills to cope with the frequent and often forceful conflicts that characterize recess. While helpful, such efforts fail to address the impact of the violence vendors in the entertainment industry.

This truth recently struck me while watching the film *Indiana Jones and the Last Crusade*. The innumerable deaths portrayed in the film—so unrealistic in terms of the circumstances surrounding them—prompted laughter from me and the rest of those in the theater. The ripping violence surrounding the deaths was lost somehow in the "humor." We have been brought to the place where a thing is not evil if it seems ludicrous enough.

Rock music has been a favorite whipping boy of conservative Americans since Elvis appeared on the Ed Sullivan show in the mid-fifties. But the hedonistic road out of the sixties found expression in ways other than just rock music. The Supreme Court decision in *Roe v. Wade*, the household buzz-word of evangelicals in the eighties, was more than just a political move by feminists and liberals. It was the seventies' counterpart of Enovid's release of "the pill" in the late sixties. For the first time in history, the birth control pill allowed females to enjoy pleasure without responsibility, a luxury formerly reserved for American males.

Roe v. Wade further separated pleasure from responsibility, especially for the female. The vast majority of abortions performed annually in the United States are for birth control reasons, not to "spare the victims of poverty, rape, and incest from further pain," the emotional platform from which militant pro-choice proponents preached in 1973. Abortion on demand is another of the enduring legacies of the sixties' sexual ethic turned inward and is a supreme form of hedonism: insisting that another must die as a consequence of my desire for personal pleasure.

"BE ALL THAT YOU CAN BE"

Many of the growing expressions of hedonism were subtle, even seemingly helpful, in their appeal. The early seventies saw the release of numerous books focusing on the self, such as Robert Ringer's *Winning Through Intimidation* and *Looking Out for Number One*, Wayne Dyer's *Your Erroneous Zones* and *Pulling Your Own Strings*, and Sherwin Cotler's *Assertion Training*. The seventies saw the birth of *Self* magazine and paved the way for the current obsession with popular psychology.

Hedonism has become so entrenched in the American psyche that feelings (the barometers of pleasure) and self (the recipient of pleasure) are the two most pampered and pandered items on nearly every agenda, from advertising to business and education. Satisfied Toyota owners boast, "I love what you do for me." Mazda encourages us to buy their vehicles because "It just feels right." Revlon taunts, "Nothing so sensual was ever so innocent" in promoting Jontue cologne. Clairol boasts that their hair color, Nice 'n Easy, is one of the "simple things" that "make you feel best."

This spotlight on self has even muscled its way into our national security. No longer should one enter the armed forces because of a patriotic duty but rather to "be all that you can be . . . in the army!"

Another chronicler of America's post-sixties migration toward hedonism is the doll Mattel promotes as representing everything every little girl hopes to be, Barbie. In 1962, Barbie got her first car, an Austin Healy—pink, of course. It was sporty yet modest. But by 1974, Barbie had acquired, among other things, a three-story townhome complete with private elevator. In 1977, she was sporting a Corvette convertible and a large motor home. By 1981, Barbie's Corvette had acquired a cellular phone, TV, and glitter accents. Today, Barbie's car is a $150,000 Ferrari 328—red, of course.[6]

One of my six-year-old twin daughters stumbled onto the issue of our nation's passion for pleasure in one of those arguments among children that parents are rarely privileged to overhear. Her friend insisted, "Barbie's a good doll! She just likes nice things." To which my daughter, known more for her candor than her compassion, retorted, "Barbie's just selfish!"

Unfortunately, Barbie is more than a children's toy. She stands as a symbol for much of what we have become. From every billboard, TV ad, and direct-mail package comes the message that the particular product will either make you feel better, provide some sexual gratification, or improve your image.

We see the offspring of hedonism all around us. The recent moral collapse of "televangelism" due to the impropriety of some within its ranks, the pleasure-seeking blunders of prominent politicians, the rise of deviant sexual behavior, the staggering numbers of teen pregnancies, and the epidemic of drug and alcohol abuse among our youth all point to an indulgent society where temperance and self-control are considered archaic and passé.

Hedonism was a close relative of irrational optimism—both sought to forget the past and construct some alternative way of life. People who took a third road out of Dodge would concur with Solomon that hedonism and optimism, and everything else "under the sun," was vanity. For them, the answers to life's deepest dilemmas seemed to lie somewhere above or beyond the sun, along the road called mysticism.

NOTES

1. Stuart Goldman writes in "That Old Devil Music," *National Review*, February 24, 1989, p. 31: "[Rock-and-roll] died in 1977 with its first god, Elvis Presley. What exists today is something else—a cheap imitation of the original model. In place of the musical vitality that inspired the pioneers, there is now merely the debased desire to shock and titillate. George Orwell, in his essay on Salvador Dali, "Benefit of Clergy," described the process whereby an artist solves the problem of his meager or failing talent. In doing so, he described the recent history of rock."

2. See Bob Larson, *Rock* (Wheaton, Ill.: Tyndale, 1989), p. 132.

3. The phenomenon of hedonism-as-religion has been given a thrust of incalculable proportions by MTV (Music Television), which combines the spell-binding effect of high-tech video with the normal mesmerizing effect of rock music. It has become a primary vehicle for all that is bad in rock.

4. Stuart Goldman, "That Old Devil Music," p. 29.

5. This phenomenon was the topic of John Ellis, "Computer Games and Aggressive Behavior: A Review of the Literature," *Educational Technology*, February 1990, pp. 37-39.

6. Cynthia Robbins, *Barbie: Thirty Years of America's Doll* (Chicago/New York: Contemporary, 1989), p. 5.

No one could have predicted the consequences that the void at the heart of the nations would produce. But philosopher Blaise Pascal had foreseen, three centuries earlier, the chilling consequences. He argued that in a spiritual vacuum, men can pursue only two options: first, to imagine that they are gods themselves, or second, to seek satisfaction in their senses.

Charles Colson
Kingdoms in Conflict

I had forced untimely access to the "source of life." . . . I recognized too late that murky elements had taken a hand. I got to know them after they already had too much power. There was no way back. I now had the world of spirits I had wanted to see. The demons came up from the abyss.

Karl Jaspers
General Psychopathology

8

THE SKY'S NO LIMIT!

The escape routes of irrational optimism and hedonism avoided the basic questions about life and truth, the emblems of the sixties' counterculture ideology, by turning their focus from ultimate to immediate concerns. A third response to the collapse of the sixties' counterculture continued to seek answers, but not in the material world. This response basically said, "We asked all the heavy questions, but we couldn't find any answers. Therefore, we need to look outside of ourselves for the answers."

Those responding this way to the sixties' failure walked right up to the threshold of the historic Christian faith. Unfortunately, because the institutional church was perceived as part of the despised "system," and had neither taken the counterculture seriously nor offered any significant model of authentic biblical faith, most of the refugees from the decade looked elsewhere for answers. And there were plenty to be found! New spiritual philosophies and organizations multiplied in the seventies. Consider this partial listing:

1969: David Berg founded the Children of God cult, offering a perversion of orthodox Christianity combined with Hindu doctrines. By 1977, Berg claimed a membership of six thousand in eight hundred colonies in more than seventy countries.[1]

1969: Anton LaVey's Satanic Bible was published.

1971: Guru Maharaj Ji, the thirteen-year-old "master," arrived in the United States. Within two years, 480 of his Divine Light Mission centers existed worldwide, and the group claimed 38,000 members in the United States alone.

1971: Victor Paul Weirwille, founder of the Way International, hosted the Rock of Ages Christian Music Festival in New Knoxville, Ohio. There were one thousand in attendance. A second concert four years later drew 8,300 at $25 a seat.[2] A central belief in the theology of the Way was stated clearly in the title of one of Weirwille's key books: *Jesus Christ Is Not God.*

1971: Jim Jones' Peoples Temple began gaining public attention as it moved to a larger building in San Francisco. Jones achieved his final, tragic notoriety in 1978 when he led nearly nine hundred of his members to mass suicide in the jungles of Jonestown in South America.

1972: The International Society for Krishna Consciousness (ISKCON), a slightly Westernized version of classical Hinduism, had nearly seventy centers in the United States and abroad and claimed a circulation of 300,000 for their magazine, *Back to Godhead.* Young men in orange saffron robes and women in saris populated most major U.S. airports, chanting "Hare Krishna" and selling ISKCON literature.

1972: Maharishi Mahesh Yogi, the founder of transcendental meditation (TM), revealed his World Plan, with the stated goal of one TM instructor for every one thousand people in the world.

1972: Korean "messiah" Sun Myung Moon, founder of the Unification Church (a combination of Buddhism and Christianity), arrived in the United States. Within a few years, flower peddlers (known as Moonies) were on countless U.S. street corners as his primary fund-raising tool.

New cults seemed to appear almost daily after the collapse of the sixties' counterculture. One group dedicated to educating Christians about these cults, the Spiritual Counterfeits Project, claimed in 1979, "There are an estimated 2,000-3,000 aberrant social-religious fringe groups in this country, composed of deeply committed and sometimes fanatical members.³ Many already established metaphysical and religious organizations suddenly experienced an unprecedented hearty welcome from American culture, particularly the youth. Groups such as Eckankar, Scientology, "est," and the Church Universal and Triumphant proselytized and published to open hearts and minds. Young people rushed headlong to them, looking for answers and a sense of belonging.

The often bizarre aspects of these new religions, culminating with the grisly television documentaries from Jonestown, tended to eclipse the more subtle yet permanent migration that was occurring away from the Judeo-Christian worldview toward what has become a nearly wholesale acceptance of the monism ("everything is God") characteristic of Eastern religions.

This "Go east, young man" mentality also made serious and lasting inroads into the music of the era. Ritchie Blackmore, of Deep Purple fame, was involved in soul travel and recorded a song entitled "Yoga for Health." The rock group Yes's album, *Tales from Topographic Oceans*, was based on the Hindu scriptures. Seals and Croft were outspoken promoters of the universalistic Baha'i faith. Pete Townshend of the Who became involved with an Eastern guru.

Ex-Beatle George Harrison became deeply involved in Eastern religions about this time. His song "My Sweet Lord" was dedicated to Lord Krishna of Hinduism. He wrote the foreword to one of the key books given away by the Hare Krishna movement. Even "country boy" John Denver made the short metaphysical journey from the irrational to the suprarational in the mid-seventies, endorsing Werner Erhard's est (Erhard seminar training), as well as the teachings of Swami Muktananda Paramahansa.

The serious involvements of the Beach Boys and the Beatles with TM founder Mahareshi Mahesh Yogi become significant in this larger context. The East had indeed come West—and it was here to stay.

The current popularity of TM, astrology, holistic health, channeling, and other metaphysical delicacies, under the innocuous umbrella of the New Age movement, results largely from the fact that spiritually fallow ground was tilled deeply in the seventies, in response to the previous decade's empty promises.

JOURNEY INTO THE OCCULT

Eastern religious ideologies were not the only spiritual beneficiaries of the sixties' failure. The occult in all its garish garments marched out of the closet and into the open arena of respectability during this same period. Anton LaVey, founder of the Church of Satan in San Francisco in 1966 and author of *The Satanic Bible* and *The Satanic Rituals*, became a celebrity. He claimed that he and his followers were merely modern paganists, not devil-worshipers.

America's new fascination with the occult side of the supernatural was evidenced in 1970 when *Man, Myth and Magic: An Illustrated History of the Supernatural* sold more than one million copies in its first edition.[4] It still stands tall on the shelves of most American libraries. During the 1976 Christmas season, Avalon Hill, noted for its military strategy games, released the Witchcraft Ritual Kit, and the Black Magic Ritual Kit for children. These board games were complete with instructions for casting spells and summoning spirits. The outside of one box teased, "Does witchcraft really work? Perform the rituals in the intimacy of your own home, with a loved one or friend and find out for yourself." Ouija boards, which had been available in stores for years, seemed innocent by comparison.

As would be expected, experimenting with the metaphysical also became a dominant theme in much of the rock music of the same era. Groups like Black Sabbath, Blue Oyster Cult, the Rolling Stones, Led Zepplin, the Eagles, and numerous others were suddenly singing songs about Satan, suicide, and demons, and extolling the value of witchcraft and soul travel.[5]

Since the early seventies, satanists and other purveyors of occult goods and services have enjoyed the popularity of quasi-religious leaders. In 1989, Rhode Island officially recognized witchcraft as a religion, entitled to all the benefits that accompany that status. In 1987, Time-Life Publishers released *Mysteries of the Unknown*, a book similar to the 1970 *Man, Myth and Magic* series. This seven-volume set deals with psychic powers, apparitions, UFOs, psychokinesis, visions, and mystical places. Checking our local library's holdings, I was concerned to discover that thirty of the forty-one copies of the books in the series were checked out.

Because of its genuine connection to ultimate evil, the dark side of the occult cannot remain hidden or masked forever. Law enforcement agencies and care professionals are beginning to take the harsh realities of satanism more seriously. Hartgrove Hospital in Chicago recently initiated a treatment program for teenagers involved in satanic cults. Other hospitals around the country are considering launching similar programs because of the severity and complexity of the mental, emotional, and physical trauma often associated with satanism.[6] Law enforcement and investigative personnel are beginning to connect abductions and missing persons reports with occult groups and practices. But unfortunately, though general interest in the occult is high, the overall attitude of our country towards the dangers of occultism is indifference and apathy.

The legacy of this fascination and involvement in the occult during the seventies has been a sort of "spiritual lobotomy." Today, many are unable to discern what is evil, and as a result, unwilling to judge anyone else's "spiritual preferences." This rise of interest in occultism, coupled with a relative tolerance toward obviously harmful occult practices, parallels what the sixties' sexual revolution did to our nation's attitudes about sexual perversion.

THE JESUS MOVEMENT

Eastern and occultic ideologies were not the only ones that benefited from the demise of the counterculture agenda. The Jesus Movement of the late sixties and early seventies had a major affinity to conservative Christianity. However, its impact must be evaluated in light of this larger spiritual context.

In 1971, *Christianity Today* released a special publication, *A News Diary of the Jesus Revolution from the Pages of Christianity Today*. The introduction to the magazine captured the sentiment of many conservative Christian leaders of the era, who had been following American youth with great interest:

> A tidal wave of revival and outreach has crashed into the world's scene, splashing into every continent, touching many nations, transforming the lives of hundreds of thousands of persons within the past few years. Throughout the world, it's known as the Jesus Revolution.
>
> When did it begin? Who is involved? Why the fantastically rapid spread? What are its hallmarks? How does it manage to span the gaps between generations and even cultures? What does it all mean? Is it biblical? Will it last?
>
> . . . We are convinced that the Holy Spirit is at the center of the worldwide Jesus Revolution. These representative accounts form an exciting diary that reads much like a modern version of the book of Acts.[7]

With the benefit of hindsight, we can approach such sweeping statements cautiously. Some "Jesus freaks" turned from drugs to Jesus, and then either back to drugs or on to some other "high." Some, as noted earlier, even tried to bring their drugs into Christianity. Another weakness of the Jesus movement was its seeming lack of significant social reform. Like the larger culture, its emphasis was often on the self, at the expense of the other-directedness of biblical faith.[8] I do not belittle the enormous wave of interest in conservative Christianity or deny that true Christian conversions occurred during the late sixties and early seventies. But an understanding of that phenomenon demands an acquaintance with and integration of the larger truth: The sixties failure produced a spiritual vacuum of incredible proportions, which overwhelmed American youth. There was a revival of huge proportions during this time, but the Jesus revolution should be seen merely as one slice of a much larger spiritual pie.

As with the other two strains of mystical investigation, popular music played an important role in the spread of the Jesus movement. Early Christian-rock artists like Larry Norman, Randy Stonehill, the Rez Band, and Randy Matthews sought to bring Christian values and a biblical worldview into the music of American youth. They encountered incredible opposition from many within the conservative community. The persistence and patience of the musicians in those difficult early years is probably the most significant reason that contemporary Christian music has become a multi-million-dollar industry today. That is not to say that all contemporary Christian music is good and beneficial to the kingdom of God. But any who enjoy the talents of Amy Grant, Sandi Patti, Michael W. Smith, and a host of others who occupy the airwaves of Christian radio have a debt to the Christian "radicals" of the late sixties and early seventies.

The three roads out of Dodge taken by the disenchanted refugees of the collapsed counterculture—irrational optimism, hedonism, and mysticism—were well traveled and have been well maintained. Their intersections with one another and the resulting byways are with us today beneath the umbrella of "pluralism." These avenues of escape from the sixties have evolved beyond mere behaviors or philosophies, and have become a comprehensive ideology that has saturated the worldview of most of today's American youth.

Our larger culture may refuse to allow us to question the validity of these philosophical, spiritual, and sexual tangents. But we must understand where they came from and why so that we may be able to know what to do with them now that they are here—and now that they are placing an entire generation at risk.

NOTES

1. Joseph M. Hopkins, "A Comparison of Teachings," *SCP Newsletter*, July-September 1980, pp. 7-9.
2. Allan Wallerstedt, *Victor Paul Weirwille and The Way* (Berkeley, Calif.: Spiritual Counterfeits Project, 1976), pp. 4-5.
3. "Introduction," *SCP Journal*, September 1979, p. 4.
4. Os Guinness, *Encircling Eyes* (Downers Grove, Ill.: InterVarsity, 1974), p. 36.
5. Bob Larson, *Rock* (Wheaton, Ill.: Tyndale, 1989), pp. 39-46. The Eagles derived their name from a spirit in the Indian religion. They also were avid fans of mystical writer Carlos Castenada. Blue Oyster Cult's album jackets were studded with religious imagery such as churches, Bibles, and hearses. Black Sabbath's two album titles say much: *Sabbath Bloody Sabbath* and *We Sold Our Soul for Rock and Roll*. The *Sabbath Bloody Sabbath* cover features a nude person in the midst of what appears to be a cult ritual. The bedpost has engraved upon it "666." The Rolling Stones' songs "Sympathy for the Devil" and "Dancing with Mr. D." and the album title, *Their Satanic Majesties Request*, make clear satanic statements. In fact, the album *Goat's Head Soup*, which contains the song "Dancing with Mr. D.," was partially recorded in Haiti during a voodoo ritual. One cannot dismiss this as the idle pastime of a few fringe groups. Many of these performers were (or are) mainline popular musicians.
6. Ken Sidey, "The Horror and the Hype," *Christianity Today* (November 17, 1989), p. 50.
7. "Introduction," *A News Diary of the Jesus Revolution from the Pages of Christianity Today* (Washington, D. C.: Christianity Today, 1971), p. 2.
8. Noted nineteenth-century revivalist Charles Finney maintained that true spiritual revival is always accompanied by visible social reform. See Charles Finney, *Lectures on Revivals of Religion* (Boston: Harvard U., 1960). See also Donald Dayton, *Discovering an Evangelical Heritage* (New York: Harper & Row, 1976), pp. 15-24. This church historian makes a sound argument for Finney's position.

Part 2

AGE OF AQUARIUS
or
EVE OF DESTRUCTION?

I liked the outlook of these children of the "Age of Aquarius." While they were arrogant and haughty, they did seem to have the right kinds of dreams. As a matter of fact, in their idealism I found the values that I wished were more evident in the churches I attended and served. There was something noble about their visions of the future, and those of us committed to a radical theology of the Kingdom of God began to think that these young people were more Christian than most of those who filled the pews of churches.

Tony Campolo
Who Switched the Price Tags?

9

THE WORLDVIEW OF THE SIXTIES

The sixties have earned a shroud of nostalgia—that convenient blurring of facts that enshrines people, events, and eras more than reality warrants. The enduring affection for the sixties is evidenced in the popularity of television series like "The Wonder Years" and "Thirtysomething." One reason for their success is the fact that the majority of Americans living today retain significant memories from that era. And for boomers now in middle age, the sixties have become a fond, albeit distorted, memory of a season when life was good—the "remember whens" of countless "happy hour" conversations. Unaware of the disastrous philosophical connections between their own time of youth and that of their children, they maintain a spectator role, watching the plight of young people instead of sensing any responsibility that would demand personal involvement.

The sixties was indeed the "decade that would not die, the decade whose long half-life continues to contaminate our own."[1] The more we understand of that era—its hopes, dreams, disasters, and pain—the better we will understand how and why the present generation came to be at risk. Perhaps then we can determine how to help those within its ranks.

The sixties has been called a "hinge in history" because so much changed as a result. It was the functional pivot for two generations. In many ways, the sixties generation owed its orientation and ideology to the forties generation. The boomers were a reaction to their parents and what they stood for. In like fashion, the kids of the nineties owe their orientation and ideology to the sixties generation, only this time as a consequence rather than a reaction.

Four Firm Beliefs

The sixties was a mosaic of groups and individuals occupying a shared moment in time. But within that diversity, there was also a significant unity. There were some common denominators, a sort of subcultural tribal ethic, within the various ideologies represented among the black community, the Left, and the flower children. This shared outlook contained four common beliefs that were evident in varying degrees among all who populated the youth culture. One of the most important had to do with their perspective of people.

AN OBLIGATION TO CARE

In the sixties, there was a common conviction that people were important: other people, to be more specific. An altruistic spirit seemed to permeate the youth. They opened their apartments, shared their food, loaned their vehicles, and gave of their money. The phenomenon of hitchhiking, the accepted mode of movement, demonstrated this fact. It was the countercultural equivalent of a mortal sin to drive past a hitchhiker if you had room in your car.

Deep in our hearts we really *wanted* to care for others. It was important to us. A friend and I once fixed a hot breakfast for a drunk who showed up on our doorstep. The thought of turning him away never entered our minds. I often wonder what might have happened if *Roe v. Wade* had occurred in 1963 instead of ten years later. The near obsession of the sixties' youth with the rights of the oppressed and disenfranchised may have solicited a verdict opposite to the one rendered in the seventies—a time when it was in vogue to be selfish.

This vague sense of obligation to care extended beyond dealings with people to include nature. There awakened a sense of responsibility to protect the environment, a desire to preserve and care for their new mother—nature. Even the current bumper sticker "Love Your Mother—Earth" has its roots nearly two decades back.

THE VALUE OF THE INDIVIDUAL

The sixties' worldview also embraced the importance of the individual to effect change. The tribal belief among most American youth was that they, as individuals, were needed for lasting social change. They believed each person could accomplish something significant and permanent. This stands in stark contrast to the overwhelming sense of impotence most American youth feel today.

The greenhouse effect, large-scale poverty, and the threat of nuclear war all seem distant and uncontrollable to most of today's teenagers. But in the sixties, youth believed that each person could make a difference. The fact that there were millions of us bolstered our hopes of how successful we could be. In his book on the era, *Dreams Die Hard*, author David Harris spotlighted this conviction in a comment about Allard Lowenstein, a mentor for some in the Left: "He argued that one person can make an immense difference and that the course of history itself could be shaped by a single decision. . . . . Everyone should take his life seriously, he urged, and devote it to worthy efforts."[2]

The involvement of whites in the Mississippi Summer Project in the early sixties, the participation of youth in the Peace Corps, and the willingness to become involved in other social needs were evidences of a vision and belief that one person could do substantial good. This became the source of a feeling of significance and self-worth for the youth of the

generation. Their sense of identity was wrapped up in helping others and believing it was worthwhile. The fervency of
this ideology led, of course, to a tremendous sense of loss in
the early seventies, when it appeared that the efforts of so
many had been in vain.

TOGETHER WE CAN CHANGE THE WORLD

A third important facet of the worldview of youth in the
sixties was actually a corollary of the second: Together we
can change the world! This belief provided a sense of hope. It
was one thing to want to help others, or to believe that one
individual could help another, but the larger concept of actually changing history had tremendous appeal.

Collier and Horowitz speak of this sense of being on the
edge of creating history: "This was part of the decade's transcendental conviction that there was something apocalyptic
lurking behind the veil of the ordinary, and that just a little
more pressure was needed to pierce the last remaining mem-
brane—of civility, bourgeois consciousness, corporate liberalism, sexual uptightness, or whatever else prevented us all
from breaking through to the other side.[3]

Any effort, any sacrifice, any cost would be gladly given
by the generation that believed they could stop poverty, racism, and war simply by telling it to go away.

THE PLASTIC SOCIETY

One conviction of the sixties' youth, however, held sway
over the others, because it conveyed the idea of urgency. The
belief that they could change history depended upon this
fourth facet of their worldview, namely that American culture *needed* to be changed. The final plank in the ideological
platform of most American youth in the sixties was that the
system, the authority conglomerate of home, church, education, and government, was intrinsically and hopelessly ill.

A great hollow in the soul of our nation was perceived
by the youth at the end of the Eisenhower era. Filling this

void occupied a central place in most of their minds. In the sixties' movie *The Graduate*, a successful businessman tries to lure recent college graduate Dustin Hoffman into cozy middle-class materialism with a hot tip for success: invest in "plastics." That businessman summarized America's future in a single word, *plastics*, and thus captured the heartbeat of youth. "Plastic" became a catchword for the larger perceived malady in America. It conjured up images of greed fueled by opportunity, lucrative lifestyles, and a superficial existence. The system, the institutions responsible for manufacturing and maintaining this plastic society, had to go.

Seeking an answer to why the hippie lifestyle and ideology were becoming so popular, *Time* magazine saw a connection to the larger culture's anemia:

> This vanguard of hippies was only the most tangible symbol of a new philosophy that cut to the very core of American life. For the first time in the nation's history, its basic Protestant ethic of hard work, respectability and competition for material success had been called massively to account. An entire generation—not only the love children, but the millions of young people who copied their clothing, hair styles, rock music and their general outlook—seemed to have found it wanting.[4]

The baby boomers had audited America and concluded that those in management of the nation were incompetent. David Harris concurred in his recollection of the motivation behind the activities of the era:

> We all wanted to become "human," "aware," "honest," and "true to our beliefs," traits few of our elders seemed to possess. We all believed the war mirrored everything wrong with America. We all, to one degree or another, found a discredited America impossible to reconcile with who we wanted to be. . . . The society we were expected to adhere to had been so thoroughly compromised, we said, that it now demanded an entirely new formulation. We believed we were laying the foundations of a New Age.[5]

This conviction that the parent culture was artificial and dishonest, that it had substituted materialism for love, propelled the beliefs of the sixties' worldview.

YOUNG REBELS

These four convictions dominated the worldview of the sixties' youth culture. They were the ideologies carried by political activist and flower child alike, and the motivation behind much of the moral mischief and social mayhem. Yet, thanks mostly to the media, this qualitative dimension of the era was totally eclipsed by another, more marketable feature: the rebellion visible in the lifestyle of most counterculture youth. This primal belief that American society in all its forms and features was selfish and artificial became license for lewdness. The cohabiting, "free love," music, drug use, and outlandish costumes of the suburban rebels of the sixties were evidences of the antithetical stance of American youth.

Yet, there was something genuine about the sixties' youth. It was more than the "youthful idealism" that educators love to pontificate about. There was a genuine dissatisfaction with American life and values as they were perceived. But the metaphysical longings did not attract viewers on the nightly news—riots, sex, drugs, and body counts for each day of the war did. Consequently, the American public received a steady, carefully edited version of the decade. There were riots, love-ins, sit-ins, bombs, murder, and chaos in the sixties. But what percentage of the youth population was actually involved in these events?

While speaking on this subject recently, I queried the audience. Everyone responded that they were aware of what went on in the sixties, but only a handful had actually participated or observed firsthand. Most had received their knowledge by way of the television in their living room. The unfortunate consequence was that the basic ideology behind the rebellion was never given consideration. It is the activities of the sixties that will live on in infamy. Even the "social awareness" films like *Easy Rider, Joe,* and *Woodstock* were merely attempts of enterprising opportunists. They made money by promenading the counterculture lifestyle on film—minus the ideology.

We must recognize the largely positive belief system beneath the behavior, while admitting that much of the resulting behavior was excessive and wrong. This is vital in order to fully appreciate the devastation that occurred when the sixties' agenda collapsed, but even more so to understand the 180 degree turn the youth made in the seventies. The direction they took as the sixties collapsed blazed the trail our children walk today.

NOTES

1. Peter Collier and David Horowitz, *Destructive Generation: Second Thoughts About the Sixties* (New York: Summit, 1989), p. 15.

2. David Harris, *Dreams Die Hard* (New York: St. Martins/Marek, 1982), p. 97. Harris was born in 1946, putting him in the "first wave" of baby boomers. He was one of the early radicals involved in the civil rights causes in the South. He was active in the development of the Mississippi Freedom Party and other attempts to secure black voting rights.

3. Collier and Horowitz, *Destructive Generation*, p. 14.

4. *This Fabulous Century*, vol. 7 (Alexandria, Va.: Time-Life, 1970), p. 59.

5. Harris, *Dreams Die Hard*, p. 142.

To emphasize the meaninglessness of the whole, by explication or implication, is to force either total pessimism or unwarranted egocentricity on the lonely particular, man. He becomes, in modern terminology, consumption centered— no longer creative and productive, but concerned essentially with getting his share out of the whole meaningless mess.

Rousas J. Rushdoony
Intellectual Schizophrenia

10

THE MAN IN THE MIRROR

The warm feelings of the peace movement, the sense of love propagated by the hippie lifestyle, and the illusion of coherence manufactured at Woodstock were not enough to materialize the Aquarian Dream. Even though the diagnosis of the culture had been accurate, the prognosis wasn't. The counterculture had drawn a circle around all that was wrong with America, only to discover that they were inside the circle!

As time progressed, some who tried to hang onto the counterculture banner discovered that it was dripping with blood. Collier and Horowitz, realizing the damage done by the antiwar efforts alone, concluded:

> The government we had sought to undermine might not be able to punish us, but history would not prove so kind. In the years after America's defeat in Vietnam, we were presented with a balance sheet showing the sobering consequences of our politics. New Left orthodoxy had scorned the idea that the war was about North Vietnamese aggression and Soviet expansion, but soon after the American pullout, North Vietnamese armies were in Cambodia and Laos, and the Russians were occupying the bases at Cam Ranh Bay and Da Nang and securing exploitation rights to natural resources in Indochina

in unmistakably imperial style. What we had dismissed as impossible was happening with dizzying speed. . . . In Cambodia, two million peasants died at the hands of the Communist Khmer Rouge, protégés of Hanoi and beneficiaries of the New Left's "solidarity" with the revolutionary cause. It was a daunting lesson: more people had been killed in the first two years of the Communist peace than in the thirteen years of America's war.[1]

Paralleling this confession, a friend recently confided in me that the atrocities of the Khmer Rouge had transformed him in short order from an adherent of the radical Left ideology to a patriotic conservative. But for many of us, it would take another fifteen years—until our own children approached adolescence—before we would realize the devastating consequences of unraveling a nation's moral, spiritual, and political fiber.

In response to the crushing disillusionment of the early seventies, the youth of the sixties began to turn inward for emotional survival. MIT psychologist Kenneth Keniston, commenting on the contrast between the eras, said, "They're turning much more inwardly to their own psyches—something we seldom saw in the sixties when youth was turning outward to change society."[2]

No More "Brothers and Sisters"

In high irony, the generation that began by promoting selflessness and sacrifice slowly transformed into one that valued the intimate self and introspection. Yet at the same time, it is understandable. The abuse of drugs, the emphasis on Eastern religious experiences, and the conviction that there was more to reality than what the five senses reported, all helped to sharpen the coming focus on self. American youth gradually found themselves mesmerized and eager to travel the inner road for personal fulfillment and self-gratification. The outer reality of oppressed others had gone rancid.

Sandwiched between the attempt on her life and her own suicide, Fay Stender, one-time militant activist for social change, pronounced an anathema on altruism that became the unconscious motto of an entire generation: "I would never again make the mistake of doing something for somebody else's benefit."³ Meanwhile, leftist guru Abbie Hoffman announced this bitter summation: "I know one thing, I don't use the phrase 'brothers and sisters' much anymore, except among real close friends, and you'll never hear me use the word 'movement' except in a sarcastic sense."⁴

Altruism had given way to antipathy. As the "you" decade slipped quietly into the "me" decade, it gave birth to the "me generation," the children of the seventies.

When reality foreclosed on the bankrupt counterculture, three outstanding debts remained. Because the sixties generation failed to provide a genuine counterculture, American youth, particularly those born in the sixties, did not receive the social inheritance traditionally passed on by a *bona fide* culture—the external basis for truth, personal meaning, and morality. Without these prerequisites for meaningful life, a vacuum developed that had a devastating effect on the larger culture, especially among today's youth.

Probably the most serious effect was that altruism wasted away. In the sixties, people were marching and protesting for the rights of others. It really didn't matter who those others were if the cause seemed legitimate. Today, we are virtually overwhelmed with private interest groups all fighting for the largest possible slice of the American pie.

The popularity of the menagerie collectively known as the "New Age movement" is evidence of the inward focus on self. The main tenet of this phenomenon is that individual man is god—the zenith of self-absorption. There can be no greater preoccupation with self than to build a shrine in your own honor and pay homage. Even the renewed interest in the occult sciences is merely the dark side of a preoccupation with self—the quest to enhance personal power.

Undoubtedly, some will disagree with this description of baby-boom Americans and point to involvement in Greenpeace, Live Aid, recycling, AIDS relief, Earth Day, and other benevolent causes. But if you peel away the veneer, we still appear to be committed to issues and ideas, not people.

This past Thanksgiving, our children asked if they could serve the homeless instead of enjoying a home-cooked meal. My wife and I decided it would be a great thing to do. We all signed up to work at a special dinner given by an inner-city church. I spent my time cutting meat in the kitchen while the kids served tables and Jill worked on the food line.

I was joined by a young coed from a prestigious local private college. We began to talk. She said most of her friends were too "self-absorbed," and that she wanted to "do something for someone else" this Thanksgiving. But after staying only forty-five minutes and interacting with no one, my young altruist left. I'm sure that later her friends all heard of her selfless act. But none had the advantage of knowing that while she was at the church, her life never actually intersected with another individual for even a second. She never made the connection that defines shared pain and challenges us with the question of whether we will become involved or merely intrigued. She was committed to the idea of compassion, motivated by the need for compassion, but far removed from the reality of compassion. She is not unlike many of us who have become comfortable sending our "involvement" through the mail in the form of monthly checks, while maintaining a sort of sterilized distance from the reality of individual human pain.

This "global vs. immediate" principle is illustrated by women contemplating abortion who change their minds upon seeing a first or second trimester fetus with their own eyes. Suddenly, the issue of abortion has a mooring to the real world of people and things; in this case, babies. It's not simply a matter of "choice" any longer, because they have traveled the short distance from "issue" to "individual."

Modern psychology has shifted greatly to accommodate our culture's love affair with the mirror. We are now told that in order to be truly healthy, we must first love ourselves and heal our own problems. Allan Bloom, in his controversial book *The Closing of the American Mind*, made a rather scathing attack on the modern notion of health and self:

> The great change is that a good man used to be the one who cares for others, as opposed to the man who cares exclusively for himself. Now the good man is the one who knows how to care for himself, as opposed to the man who does not. . . . Of course, we are told, the healthy inner-directed person will really care for others. To which I can only respond: If you can believe that, you can believe anything.[5]

Bloom maintains that the self has become the modern substitute for the soul.[6] Interest in the things of the soul was laid to rest during the sixties demise, when America became obsessed with her psychic security.[7] Even the very real spiritual revival that was discussed in chapter 8 needs to be understood in terms of a trend toward narcissism. The extreme dedication visible among youth in cults like ISKCON and the Moonies was motivated more by the need to fill a vacuum within than to meet a need without, in society.

MORALITY AND ETHICS

Another legacy of the sixties' failure, one which is in full flower among today's youth, is the tendency to look to self for moral absolutes. The family, the church, or society at large had previously dictated what was right and wrong, either by inference, instruction, or law. But the autonomy that began as rebellion in the sixties became ritual, and finally religion, by the seventies. The new basis for truth and morality for American youth shifted from outside man to inside him. One's personal feelings and experience governed the new morality. Ethics were by default—as the situation dictated. Like religion, they became a matter of one's private world, immune to public scrutiny and regulation.

But this shift was not the work of a single generation. Part of the blame for the moral decline of today's youth goes back much further than the sixties generation, even though they accelerated the process tremendously. One of the primary causes for the present moral emptiness is that the preceding three generations failed to pass on a satisfactory heritage of truth and morality to their children.

In the late nineteenth century and early twentieth century, most Americans based their moral standards on the Bible. Even with the rise of liberalism and Darwinism, the basic foundation for morality was the Judeo-Christian Scriptures. It was an integral part of school curriculum, and a learned man was one who had read and studied the Bible. Such was the faith of my own great-grandmother, born in 1872. But her generation passed the first of a series of smoldering torches to their children. They taught their children the precepts without the larger principles behind them. The why behind the what was never taught.

Their children grew up believing that "certain things are right or wrong, because God says so . . . somewhere." Theirs was an abiblical morality: an ethic originally based on the Scriptures, but long since loosed from its spiritual moorings.

The next generation came to the conclusion that "certain things are right and wrong, but I don't know why." They were moral people, but their morality was not anchored in the clear teachings of the Judeo-Christian Scriptures, even though it relied upon a vague memory of them. Consequently, their children were raised to play fair and work hard. But it was more because "that's what good boys do," than, "Thus saith the Lord."

My generation saw only the rules of the previous generation. When we decided to break away from the parental generation, abandoning their rules was a big part of the rebellion. The lack of connection of our personal ethic to something ultimate led easily to the next step of moral degeneration: "Certain things are right and wrong, but I don't care!"

Immorality, the conscious violation of accepted standards, was the standard of the sixties. Yet by definition, immorality still admits the existence of some standard, somewhere. But when the sixties failed and kids started looking inward for survival and solace, *feelings* about right and wrong were suddenly enthroned as absolutes. It was a small step from immorality to amorality—the prevailing principle of the next decade. The belief that no moral standards exist abides as the moral mentor of youth today. "There's no such thing as right or wrong" was the next and final cycle in the spiral away from absolutes. The accompanying chart shows the progression, or rather regression.

MORAL STANDARDS

IDEOLOGY	TIME	BELIEF
Biblical Morality	1800-early 1900s	"Certain things are right and wrong, and I know why."
Abiblical Morality	1900s-1950s	"Certain things are right and wrong, but I don't know why."
Immorality	1960-early 1970s	"Certain things are right and wrong, but I don't care!"
Amorality	late 1900s	"There's no such thing as right and wrong!"

We have become a nation ruled by instincts rather than intellect. Cal Thomas spotlighted the "respectability" given to immorality by amorality in his book *The Death of Ethics in America.* According to Thomas:

The lack of any personal accountability to a moral code has made immorality respectable in our nation. There is at times little in the press, in the entertainment industry, or in our institutions of higher (lower?) learning that can lift us up or cause us to realize that we have fallen. All of the voices are coming from below, rather than from above.[8]

If right and wrong are subjective and relative, then by default personal pleasure becomes the great moral arbiter of our nation's conscience. But pleasure is always shortsighted, willing to sacrifice the ultimate on the altar of the immediate.

The immorality of the sixties was a lot like white-water rafting—unbridled excitement, adventure in uncharted waters. But its offspring, amorality, has turned out to be like trying to raft the torrents of the sea itself. The absence of boundaries and morals has stripped life of its meaning, much like a sport without rules. Our culture's present inability to make strong moral statements in the public arena about adolescent sex, homosexuality, marital infidelity, and family disintegration stems from this moral void. Ted Koppel, host of ABC-TV's "Nightline," targeted the seriousness of this moral impotence in a recent college address:

> We have actually convinced ourselves that slogans will save us. Shoot up if you must, but use a clean needle. Enjoy sex whenever and with whomever you wish, but wear a condom. No! The answer is no.
>
> Not because it isn't cool or smart or because you might wind up in jail or dying in an AIDS ward, but because it's wrong, because we have spent 5,000 years as a race of rational human beings, trying to drag ourselves out of the primeval slime by searching for truth and moral absolutes.
>
> In its purest form, truth is not a polite tap on the shoulder. It is a howling reproach. What Moses brought down from Mt. Sinai were not the Ten Suggestions.[9]

The moral ambiguity of the eighties can be traced directly to the immorality of the sixties, when a generation decided they would be autonomous. But the failure of past generations to pass on a morality that had its roots in absolute truth must be seen as an accomplice to the crime. Teaching children how to act is a poor substitute for instructing them on how to live. But our connection to truth was not the only thing that was severed as the sixties' counterculture failed. Our culture became detached from history itself.

NOTES

1. Peter Collier and David Horowitz, *Destructive Generation: Second Thoughts About the Sixties* (New York: Summit, 1989), p. 148.
2. Quoted in Eric Fellman, "Christian Teenagers—How Do We Keep Them in Church?" *Moody Monthly* (September 1982), p. 15.
3. Collier and Horowitz, *Destructive Generation*, p. 59.
4. Abbie Hoffman, quoted from "Insight," radio program 712 (Chicago: RACOM Productions), p. 2.
5. Allan Bloom, *The Closing of the American Mind* (New York: Simon & Schuster, 1987), p. 178.
6. Ibid., p. 173.
7. Christopher Lasch, *The Culture of Narcissism* (New York: Warner, 1979), p. 33.
8. Cal Thomas, *The Death of Ethics in America* (Waco, Tex.: Word, 1988), p. 22.
9. Ted Koppel, quoted in *Youthworker Update*, December 1987, p. 8.

*Not only does democracy make every man forget his ances-
tors, but it hides his descendants and separates his contemporaries from him; it throws him back forever upon himself alone and threatens in the end to confine him to the
solitude of his own heart.*

Alexis de Toqueville
Democracy in America

*Those individuals who do not look upon themselves as a
line connecting the past with the future, do not perform
their duty to the world.*

Daniel Webster

11

A Generation Adrift

From the sixties generation the present generation has inherited self-absorption and moral relativism. The sixties' failure transformed normal adolescent egocentricity into a full-time career. The intimate self has become the primary focus of most American young people's lives. Not only has our culture nurtured its children to be consumers, but the demise of many of the foundational institutions normally associated with growing up (particularly the family) have forced young people to "look out for Number One" on grounds of self-preservation.

But there was another sixties' legacy whose bitter offspring has also permeated the souls of our youth: a preoccupation with the present. Passion, not wisdom, was the driving force of the sixties' pseudo-revolution. In our zeal for the present, we of the sixties gave little consideration to the noble, the enduring, and the right in America's history. We knew nothing of the Chinese proverb: "One generation plants the trees and the next enjoys the shade." We were ignorant of the necessity of historical continuity both in the personal and corporate spheres. Intoxicated with existentialism's appeal of creating our own "moment," we cut ourselves away from the past and felt no liability for the future.

The past was rendered irrelevant at best, evil at worst. Like an evicted tenant, our collective history was thrown into the street. Individual family histories were reduced to rubble. Ancestors and what they endured to provide the freedom that permitted rebellion were inconsequential. The present was all that mattered.

The elimination of a meaningful social genealogy created a void in the heart of the nation. The staggering success of Alex Haley's novel and TV mini-series *Roots* suggests the sobering impact of this social and historical void. In 1977, America seemed to be groping for threads to connect it to a significant past. Haley's *Roots* provided such a hope, even if it was vicarious. Noting the nation's response to the TV series, *Newsweek* commented on our scramble to find roots:

> In thousands of private homes and countless bars, in the nation's ghettos and in its whitest suburbs, it was, by proclamation and popular fancy, "Roots" week. In the midst of a numbing cold spell, Americans in near-record numbers tuned in to the story of one black man's family—and, apparently, couldn't turn it off. Appointments were canceled and parties interrupted so that people could be in front of a television set at the designated hour each night. Young children stayed up long past their bedtimes, and morning-coffee conversations recounted the latest episode. There was an atmosphere of shared experience: everyone seemed aware not only of what happened the night before but of events 200 years in the past. For eight days and nights, the most talked-about men in the country were a middle-aged writer named Alex Haley and his great-great-great-great-grandfather, Kunta Kinte.[1]

The veterans of the sixties were mesmerized by *Roots* as they relearned a simple principle: A meaningful present depends upon a meaningful past. They had despised the past, but had also neglected the future. Their utter contempt for accumulating goods, the earmark of capitalism, also blinded them to the necessity to think ahead. They foolishly assumed that the future would just happen.

By abandoning the past and neglecting the future, the counterculture generation became orphans in time. They gave birth to a myopic worldview built upon a minuscule portion of the chronological continuum: the present. But by the seventies, the results were becoming evident. Writing in 1979, Christopher Lasch pinpointed the connection between the sixties' failure and the subsequent retreat from history:

> Indeed Americans seem to wish to forget not only the sixties, the riots, the New Left, the disruptions on college campuses, Vietnam, Watergate, and the Nixon presidency, but their entire collective past. . . . To live for the moment is the prevailing passion—to live for yourself, not for your predecessors or posterity. We are fast losing the sense of historical continuity, the sense of belonging to a succession of generations originating in the past and stretching into the future. It is the waning of the sense of historical time . . . that distinguishes the spiritual crisis of the seventies.[2]

What's Happening in History Class?

The preoccupation with the present among today's youth represents a worldview that extends beyond a simple ignorance of past people, places, and events. Most young people in America also have no *appreciation* for the importance of the past. Many of their history teachers are middle-aged refugees from the sixties. An unfortunate error that is part of their sixties heritage is the overemphasis on making history "relevant" in order to maintain the interest of the students. History is always relevant, but how one goes about showing its relevance can make a serious difference.

One way to illustrate the relevance of history is to use the past to shed light on the present. With this method, the historical focus is actually the present, and the past is employed merely to show that what is happening now has happened before. This is often used to justify or condemn something or someone in the present.

A second method is to depict the present as a consequence of the past. What has happened before is shown to have a connection to the present that is more than just illustrative; it is actual. In other words, if the events of the past had been different, the present would not be the same. This method of teaching history shows students that who they are is very much a consequence of who their ancestors were. And who they are and what they do today will directly affect their own children and grandchildren.

Unfortunately, the more popular method of teaching history today is the first. As syndicated columnist George Will writes, "Today, many universities do little to equip rising generations with a sense of being legatees of a shared and valuable civilization. . . . Universities have encouraged factional disciplines, a kind of 'special interest scholarship.'"[3]

Will's concern is the thesis of Paul Vitz's recent book, *Censorship: Evidence of Bias in Our Children's Textbooks*, which reports the findings of a federally funded study he conducted at New York University in 1986.[4] Although Vitz's primary focus is the selective editing of history books to omit religious history, his research shows how history textbooks are used to teach something other than the succession of significant events. Rather than showing how past events caused present realities, those events are mentioned only if they serve to teach a lesson the textbook writer wants to teach. If the writer doesn't want to teach any lessons about religion, or if he wants to "create" a history free of religion, then religious events in history become irrelevant and are ignored.

A recent popular fictional example of this orientation towards history was the teaching style of Charlie Moore, the dynamic history teacher of a group of gifted high school students on the television sitcom "Head of the Class." Mr. Moore was always exciting, always relevant, and yet always "historical." He constantly intrigued his students by showing them how the past has tremendous relevance for today. Rather than treating history in a "linear" fashion, showing how one

event followed another, he carefully selected topics of interest for each day and artistically wove them into a captivat-
ing lesson illustrating their relevance for the present. From
the show, one got the distinct impression that history is simply the study of random events and people, organized to
teach larger principles about life.

The idea that history is linear, that it has a beginning
and an end, has become a foreign concept in academic America. However, unless history is taught as a linear phenomenon, we cannot ascribe genuine meaning to any of its random events. Unless young people see the events of history in
a causal relationship to each other, they will never understand the significance of those events, no matter how "relevantly" they are presented.

If this is true regarding the history of nations and civili-
zations, it is true of the history of individuals as well. If history has no genuine meaning, then as individuals among
countless other random people in time, we have no meaning
either. Educators who promote historical relevance at the
expense of the linear method actually undermine our young
people's own sense of relevance, purpose, and meaning. It is
impossible to teach a teenager in history class that life is a
smattering of random dots on a historical canvas, and then
turn around and tell them in psychology class that they are
somehow important and should love themselves.

Is History a Free Meal?

Today's youth are told from every angle that they have
no connection to the past. And if that is true, then they have
no responsibility to the past either—no societal debt or obligation to the culture that bore and nurtured them. Indeed,
most young people do not believe that they owe anything to
the past. Senator John Kennedy, speaking at Smith College
in 1958, captured the "old" expectations of culture that were
placed upon youth:

I ask that you offer to the political arena, and to the critical problems of our society which are decided therein, the benefits of the talents which society has helped to develop in you. I ask you to decide, as Goethe put it, whether you will be an anvil—or a hammer. . . . whether you are to give to the world in which you were reared and educated the broadest possible benefits of that education.[5]

In Kennedy's day (just forty years ago!) one was expected to give something back to the society from which he had benefited while growing up. Because there no longer exists a sense of connection to the past in the minds of our youth, any sense of the obligation Kennedy spoke of is also absent. One's social heritage is viewed as simply one more free meal. Veteran educator Rousas Rushdoony agrees, pointing out how the goals of education have changed to actually encourage this selfish view of history:

For the emphasis now is on the *needs* of the child, not on the *demands and expectations* of the culture. Once the literature of youth abounded in an emphasis on what the young man needed to know, what his spiritual armor was, what made him a complete man, a complete farmer, cobbler, or apprentice, all on the premise of his responsibility to the culture and his personal incapacity if he failed to meet the requirements of manhood and faith. . . . 'Essential' education [now] is in terms of the needs of the child, not in terms of the requirements of God and society. The consequences, of course, are children who are group-directed and consumption-centered, whose attitude toward life is one of appetite rather than responsibility.[6]

This consumerist attitude toward society is pervasive, extending even to conservative youth. The motivations behind a growing number my teen-aged students have, indeed, centered on appetite more than responsibility. Success is valued above sacrifice; the immediate is preferred to the ultimate; image is more important than substance. It has not been uncommon for students to tell me they would never enter the field of teaching because they wanted to make some "real money" or get a "real job." Yet they were willing to exploit me and other teachers to get what they wanted.

But the primary blame doesn't fall at the feet of the present generation. They have been explicitly and implicitly taught and told that the past is irrelevant in itself, and that they have no obligation to it. Today's youth have been cut off completely from any significant connection to the past. But what about the future? Does the horizon hold signs of promise for the present generation?

FUTURE TENSE

Put yourself in the emotional, psychological, and spiritual shoes of a young adult living today. Consider just three areas:

Politics. What goes through the mind of the present generation when they try to take in the "big picture" of U.S. and global politics? The Iran-Contra cover-up, U.S. senators accepting financial contributions to promote savings and loan legislation, the budget deficit, and countless other news items daily reinforce the suspicion that government cannot take care of itself, much less them! Today's youth are skeptical about America's political future. Can we blame them?

Ecology. The popular scenario created for today's teen is that earth as we know it will either slowly vaporize as the ozone layer disintegrates, starve to death as population exceeds food production, asphyxiate in a chemical smog of our own making, face extinction due to the HIV virus, or perhaps find itself as one massive toxic barge looking for a place to park. The overall message coming from educational television, science classrooms, and popular media is that planet Earth is on a collision course with destiny.

Christianity. The cumulative effect of the recent blatant deceit, misrepresentation, and rationalization of televangelists Jimmy Swaggart and Jim Bakker is probably immeasurable. The damage done to the already-diminishing reputation of conservative Christianity in the United States was staggering. At the end of the eighties, *People* magazine had a special issue, profiling "Twenty Who Defined the Decade." The list included Jim and Tammy Faye Bakker. Significantly, *People* selected humorist Dave Barry to write about Bakker. Barry's synopsis of Christian theology, television style, attests to the severe repercussions of the Bakker scandal:

> How could such a grasping, shallow and flagrantly self-absorbed couple manage to acquire such a large and fervent following? One widely accepted answer, of course, is that the followers had the same average intelligence as margarine. But I don't think that's the whole answer. I think the Bakkers were successful because they personalized a very appealing, very convenient moral philosophy that flourished in the '80s, a philosophy that can be summarized as follows: You can't do good unto others unless you feel good about yourself, and you can't feel good about yourself unless you have a lot of neat stuff. . . . . Watching the PTL Club was like watching a mutant version of Wheel of Fortune, where Pat Sajak and Vanna White won all the prizes.[7]

The public image of Christianity has been shattered for many of our youth. If identifying with Jesus Christ had been awkward or difficult for them before, it is more so now. Many other young people on the periphery of religious faith have likely directed their gaze elsewhere.

But children are resilient. They have an uncanny ability to rebound from tragedy. The private sin of public Christians might be bearable for young people if it were not also accompanied by the more devastating tragedy in a growing number of their private lives. The near epidemic of divorce among professing Christians is destroying our nation's foundation as it is perceived by the young. Each year I have taught, more and more of my students have asked for prayer for parents, aunts, uncles, brothers, and sisters facing deteriorating marriages or divorce. The pain in the lives of today's youth should become a constant reminder of the need to preserve marriage as a source of strength and hope for our children. The idea that adultery is a private sin between two consenting adults is heresy. Divorce is an attack on one of the most essential foundations in a child's world.

The future presented to today's youth is riddled with uncertainty and fear. It holds forth no certain hope. If the past is detached and irrelevant, and the future is uncertain at best and hopeless at worst, what remains? It shouldn't surprise us that many of today's youth feel hopeless. We shouldn't be shocked that they have little regard for themselves and none for the future. The rising generation is much like a massive replica of the children in William Golding's *Lord of the Flies*, where personal survival and making the most of what you have became the rudders for a shaky existence.

The nineties generation is in serious trouble. In the next section, as we probe even deeper into the roots of the present youth crisis, we'll see ever more clearly why today's youth are a generation at grave risk. Some of the things we uncover will hit close to home, as the book shifts from allowing you to remain a spectator to making you a participant in the drama.

NOTES

1. "'Roots' Takes Hold in America," *The Seventies* (New York: Newsweek, 1987), p. 27.

2. Christopher Lasch, *The Culture of Narcissism* (New York: Warner, 1979), p. 30.

3. George Will, "Universities Neglect Teaching Appreciation of Past," *The Colorado Springs Gazette Telegraph*, May 6, 1984, p. G1.

4. Paul C. Vitz, *Censorship: Evidence of Bias in Our Children's Textbooks* (Ann Arbor, Mich.: Servant, 1986). Vitz documents the unmistakable presence of leftist socialistic concepts in textbooks. In many cases, disdain for capitalism and America in general is engendered. This type of anti-conservative bias was also discovered and discussed in *What Are They Teaching Our Children?* by Mel and Norma Gabler (Wheaton, Ill.: Victor Books/Scripture Press, 1985). Peter Collier, in *Destructive Generation*, wrote about his former radical colleagues' slinking off into the teaching profession after the sixties. That influence is quite obvious in these books.

5. Quoted in Suzy Platt, ed., *Respectfully Quoted* (Washington, D. C.: Library of Congress, 1989), p. 98.

6. Rousas Rushdoony, *Intellectual Schizophrenia* (Phillipsburg, N.J.: Presbyterian & Reformed, 1961), p. 71.

7. Dave Barry, "Jim & Tammy Faye Bakker: Their Game Was Jack-in-the-Pulpit, Their Downfall a Divine Comedy of Finger Pointing," *People Weekly Extra*, Fall 1989, p. 70.

Part 3

THE AMERICAN CHURCH: A HOUSE BUILT ON SAND?

*Christian values are in retreat in the West today, primarily,
I believe, because of the church itself. If Christianity has
failed to stem the rising tides of relativism it is because the
church in many instances has lost the convicting force of
the gospel message. Earlier we argued that while human-
ists did not understand humans, Christians did not understand Christianity. This is surely evident in post World War
II Christianity, which has become a religion of private
comfort and blessing that fills up whatever small holes in
life that pleasure, money and success have left open, what
Bonhoeffer called a "god of the gaps."*

Charles Colson
Kingdoms in Conflict

12

A MIRROR IMAGE

The abiding miscarriages of hope from the sixties—the preoccupation with self and the present, and a shift in the basis for truth from external absolutes to internal feelings —have pervaded American culture. But what about evangelicalism? How has the conservative Christian church fared through this trauma? Has it remained pure and strong? Has it compromised?

Jesus Christ told believers that true disciples would be salt and light in a corrupt and dark world (Matthew 5:13-16). They were to be a genuine counterculture—a cohesive group whose values, lifestyle, and worldview differed qualitatively from the surrounding mass of humanity. British scholar John Stott, in his exposition on Matthew 5-7, describes this fundamental difference which should characterize those who claim to be Christ's disciples:

> Thus the followers of Jesus are to be different—different from both the nominal church and the secular world, different from both the religious and the irreligious. The Sermon on the Mount is the most complete delineation anywhere in the New Testament of the Christian counter-culture. Here is a Christian value-system, ethical standard, religious devotion, attitude to money, ambition, life-style and network of rela-

tionships—all of which are totally at variance with those of the non-Christian world. And this Christian counter-culture is the life of the kingdom of God, a fully human life indeed but lived out under the divine rule.[1]

Christians are to be qualitatively and noticeably distinct from the "world," those who live their lives apart from the will and wishes of God. But the question quite simply is, Are we?

Jonathan Swift wrote, "A stander-by may sometimes, perhaps, see more of the game than he that plays it."[2] As a teacher in a Christian day school for more than a decade, I have been both bystander and player. As noted in the introduction, I have counseled many of my students through the more predictable and mundane rites of adolescence, but as the years have progressed I have found myself increasingly immersed in a swamp of complex emotional, moral, and domestic problems. More and more families are falling apart. Conversations with parents reveal an alarming rise in biblical illiteracy and a growing secularization of values.

From this bystander experience, I conclude that evangelicalism in America has been gradually transformed from a counterculture to merely a subculture. Evangelical Christianity is being reduced to a mirror image of the larger culture. We embrace the same values, work for the same goals, and live for the same reasons as our nonbelieving neighbors, all the while professing that we are faithful citizens of the kingdom of God.

However, our present malaise is not simply the result of a series of selfish choices. The church didn't wake up one morning and decide it would rather be a subculture than a counterculture. Of the various expressions of the Christian faith in America, evangelicalism has had the most prolonged exposure to and conflict with the larger culture. Not wishing to accommodate the modern world as liberal expressions of Christianity have done, or hide from it like much of fundamentalism, evangelicalism sought to be conservative in its theology without being totally separatist in its lifestyle. Though attempting to be biblical, it has tried to establish an identity rooted in its affirmations rather than in mere prohibitions. Nearly fifteen years ago one theologian spotted this tendency and described it in a book entitled *The Worldly Evangelicals*. "The evangelicals knew that to influence the world for Christ, they would have to gain its attention in a positive way. In a word, they would have to become respectable by the world's standards."[3]

Unfortunately, in seeking to be respected by the larger culture while somehow being different, evangelicalism's identity slowly shifted from the absolutes of Scripture to the culture itself. Instead of faithfully deliberating over the Word of God to discover individual and corporate identity, evangelicals became infatuated with the secular culture, which resulted in an adoption of a Christianized version of secularism.

The American church has attempted to be a respected part of the world while still maintaining a safe distance from it. Unfortunately, that has proved to be like trying to maintain a safe distance between your car and the car ahead—as it drives off a pier in the fog! Or, in the words of two more recent observers, "Alas, in leaning over to speak to the modern world, we had fallen in."[4]

American secular culture is obsessed with the self, focused on the present, and steered by moral relativism. If evangelicalism has really become a mirror image of that culture, we shouldn't be surprised when we find those characteristics within the church. Yet such characteristics, engrafted from secular culture, should sound a loud alarm about American evangelicalism.

THE SELF-HELP SUPERMARKET

Nearly every bookstore in America has a section designated "Self Help." Books are available for self-improvement in nearly every conceivable area of life—even some areas most of us weren't aware of. This section in the bookstore is not simply the literary equivalent of the frozen foods section in a supermarket. It symbolizes the current secular ideology about life itself.

And how about the world of Christian books? The most recent edition of *Current Christian Books* lists nearly five hundred books whose titles begins with *How to* . . . . Suddenly, it's "biblical" to improve your sex life, balance your checkbook, lose weight, coordinate your colors, eat oat bran, break codependency, heal your past, and release your hidden personality. Growing numbers of Christians now talk about what they're "working on" in their lives. While this principle seems sound because it camps on the periphery of biblical truth, often beneath the veneer of dedication to personal change is an attitude that has much less to do with what God wants for us than with what we want for ourselves.

Former presidential aide Charles Colson perceives little distinction between the Christian subculture and the secular culture in regard to how each views the self. In speaking of the larger culture, he states:

A 1985 study titled "Habits of the Heart" calls this attitude "utilitarian individualism," arguing that the two primary ways Americans attempt to order their lives are through "the dream of personal success" and "vivid personal feeling." This was reinforced as those interviewed consistently defined their ultimate goals in terms of self-fulfillment or self-realization. Marriage was seen as an opportunity for personal development, work as a method of personal advancement, church as a means of personal fulfillment.[5]

Regarding the impact of secular society on the church and its focus, Colson continues:

What this study reflects is simply the inevitable consequences of four decades of the steady erosion of absolute values. As a result we live with a massive case of schizophrenia. Outwardly, we are a religious people, but inwardly our religious beliefs make no difference in how we live. We are obsessed with self; we live, raise families, govern, and die as though God does not exist, just as Nietzsche predicted a century ago.[6]

Colson concludes that evangelicalism's passion has shifted from God to self. The growing abundance of Christian self-help books is strong evidence in support of that forbidding conclusion.

In his classic devotional work, *My Utmost for His Highest*, Oswald Chambers says that such self-centeredness strays far from what the Christian faith should be:

> The continual grubbing on the inside to see whether we are what we ought to be generates a self-centered, morbid type of Christianity, not the robust, simple life of the child of God. . . . How long is it going to take God to free us from the morbid habit of thinking about ourselves? We must get sick unto death of ourselves, until there is no longer any surprise at anything God can tell us about ourselves. We cannot touch the depths of meanness in ourselves. There is only one place where we are right, and that is in Christ Jesus.[7]

PROFESSIONAL COUNSELING FIRST?

From 1954 to 1980, membership in the American Psychiatric Association quadrupled. During the same time period, membership in the American Academy of Child Psychology rose twenty-fold![8] A recent survey of an adult Sunday school class from a large evangelical church in our city revealed that one out of two adults either were in therapy or had been in the recent past. New Age critic and scholar Douglas Groothuis has said, "In the secularized West, psychology has replaced theology as the center of human concern."[9]

While speaking at a family conference, I made a passing comment about my concern over the church's infatuation with psychology. Afterwards, a distraught couple asked if I had time to talk with them. Their story, although painful, has become commonplace. Their small-group Bible study, once a place of vibrant study and worship, had slowly developed into an exchange of psychological clichés gleaned from therapists. In fact, this couple was the only one in their group not seeing a counselor, and the members of the group were urging them to get in therapy because of how it would help them. The group's attitude was, "You don't have to be having problems to see a therapist. He can help make a good marriage better!"

They began to wonder if perhaps they were missing the apparent benefits of modern Christian psychology. By not being in therapy, this couple had become outsiders. They were made to feel that they were outside the deeper truths about God, themselves, and life. I won't easily forget the tragic insight of a comment the woman made: "We used to sit around and share what God had said to us during the week through His Word. Now group members are only interested in sharing what their therapist told them that week about themselves."

Christian counseling is a valid and often needed ministry. We are grateful for the many professionals within its ranks. Yet how many people have gone to a Christian therapist before they have sought encouragement and guidance from God through prayer, through His Word, and through His people? It is frightening to think that the church has surrendered the custodianship of its soul to psychologists. Sadly, more than 40 percent of the degrees awarded at one leading evangelical seminary in 1990 were in counseling (rather than in theology, missions, or Christian education), and one out of three graduates took positions as counselors. This shift from theology to psychology should be a matter of concern to Christians especially because the two primary foci of modern psychology—the self and the past—are clearly earmarked in the Bible as regions that followers of Jesus Christ are to avoid or at least minimize. (See, for instance, Matthew 16:25, John 3:30, 1 Corinthians 10:24, Philippians 2:4 and 3:13-14.)

A brief tour through any Christian bookstore will verify the church's love affair with modern psychology. Counseling, psychology, and therapy-based books greatly outnumber those on theology, piety, and evangelism. More and more Christian books promise some type of "healing" of emotional damage sustained by the "victims" of a growing list of abuses. One local Christian radio station broadcast an ad from a "biblical counseling center" insisting that if the you are having difficulty with your teenager, can't get along with your in-laws, are feeling depressed, have a child struggling in school, or are fighting with your mate, you are in a "crisis" and need professional help.

At one time, many of the things we now call "problems" constituted the normal passages of parenting or growing up —the everyday fare of everyday people. And Christians believed that through the encouragement of the Scriptures, the ministry of the Holy Spirit, and a handful of caring friends they would not only "endure" but actually benefit in the long run. Unfortunately in today's church, these difficulties are packaged as "crises" from which they need to be freed, conveniently demanding the services of a "trained professional." Most Christians today have been conditioned to believe they are virtually impotent to handle the routine conflicts within their own homes much less the unfriendly and often unsavory circumstances of life in a fallen world.

Each year that I teach, the number of fifteen- to eighteen-year-olds who are or have been in therapy grows. I excuse them early or admit them late because of their appointments with counselors. They throw around words like "suppression," "dysfunctional," "self-actualization," and "co-dependent." Once the select vocabulary of a trained few, these terms are now the lunchroom banter of children.

Make no mistake, a growing number of conservative Christians in America will listen to their therapist before their pastor, and will read James Dobson and Larry Crabb before they'll read their Bible, even though neither of these men would ever wish this were the case. The evangelical community is rapidly becoming a subculture of "couch potatoes," with the couch being located in their therapist's office rather than their family room.

What has caused the American church to become so psychologically oriented and therapy centered? The most obvious reason is that we are the moral mirror image of a larger culture. And like the culture from which we were cloned, we have shifted our basis for truth and morality from external absolutes to internal feelings. Modern psychology tends to shift the focus of those involved from external to internal reality. And when internal reality becomes enthroned in the judging processes of life, disastrous things begin to happen. For one, the basis for ethics and morality shifts gradually from outside ourselves to inside ourselves. We, rather than God, have become the final authority for all areas of our personal lives.

THE VALUE OF COMMITMENT

In evangelicalism's past, the Scripture was the bedrock of life. To question its authority was tantamount to apostasy. What the Bible taught had priority over what one felt. If my opinion differed with the clear teaching of Scripture, I was obligated to promptly change my opinion. Not so anymore.

Currently, the most common and popular method of conflict resolution among Christians is simply to leave the church. Although the Bible gives the proper procedures and motives for dealing with conflict (in Matthew 5 and 18), many Christians feel free to do as they please in the arena of interpersonal relationships. This includes looking for a new church when conflict arises with the pastor or a member. In fact, many "new" churches are little more than depositories of large numbers of dissatisfied and wounded believers from other congregations. "Oh, we're still shopping," is a common response to the question, "Where do you go to church?"

Loyalty to a particular church seems to have become an outdated concept among evangelicals. Church has become merely one more item on the growing list of things that must "meet my needs—and if it doesn't, I'll take my needs elsewhere!" William Temple once remarked that the church was the only institution on earth that existed for the benefit of nonmembers. That conviction seems to have fallen out of our theological luggage somewhere along the journey.

An even more serious indication that our feelings have priority over the clear teachings of the Bible is the near epidemic level of adultery and divorce within the church. From national leaders to local pastors to the believer next door, the dissolution of marriages rages like a fire through a dry barn.

The church has responded by instituting recovery workshops, seminars, support groups, and an avalanche of books on the subject. These are all excellent ministries of compassion, but I have yet to hear a loud and clear message from the leadership within evangelicalism that divorce is sin. It is common to hear of Christians having affairs, but rarely does the word adultery appear in conversations. Even the exception clause for adultery (Matthew 19:3-9) has been interpreted by some as an encouragement to divorce rather than a last-option provision in select cases. It is more common to hear unhappily married Christians rummaging for biblical grounds for divorce than biblical grounds to remain married. The modern evangelical church asserts that it has a spiritual birthright to personal happiness. And that belief has clearly eclipsed the prior biblical mandate for personal holiness.

I do not minimize the genuine pain and trauma many Christians have suffered within an abusive marriage, or the convoluted nature of some Christians' marital histories. It is not a simple problem begging a simplistic solution. Nonetheless, the disintegration of the Christian home is the result of a diminishing sense of commitment to the God of the Bible and an increasing commitment to our own judgments in matters of truth and morality. And I believe we have yet to bring in the first full harvest of our folly. That yet awaits us in the the maturing of the present generation, our children.

A RECREATIONAL APPROACH TO PERSONAL HOLINESS

The shift from external to internal absolutes affects our entire understanding of personal holiness. Many consider God's express will that all His children live holy lives only an optional high-level commitment for a select few. Those who seem to have a passion to know, love, and please God are viewed as spiritual giants. We enjoy watching them, listening to them, and admiring them—as long as we can do so from a distance.

This represents a serious deficiency in our understanding of the nature and character of God. When man presumes to define the conditions of a covenant relationship between himself and God, he assumes he is the superior party in the transaction. In *The Gospel According to Jesus,* John MacArthur sought to awaken the church to the need for a qualitatively distinct lifestyle. However, the recent public reaction to *The Gospel* is further evidence of our insistence on defining the terms of discipleship.[10] We have convinced ourselves that discipleship is akin to low-impact aerobics; you simply set your own goal, define your pace, and work out as long as you like. "High impact" spirituality is for the few; simply being in shape is cause for satisfaction.

The modern notion of worship has been infected with this recreational holiness. Growing numbers of Christians demand that their church services be exciting, fresh, stimulating, and relevant—the basic ingredients of the entertainment industry. We have become a generation of pew-sitters waiting for the show to begin. And when the show at one church no longer maintains our interest, we simply find a better one elsewhere.

This spectator-worship is nothing new, however. In Ezekiel 33:31-32, the Old Testament prophet is commissioned by God to confront His people for this same sin:

> My people come to you, as they usually do, and sit before you to listen to your words, but they do not put them into practice. With their mouths they express devotion, but their

hearts are greedy for unjust gain. Indeed, to them you are nothing more than one who sings love songs with a beautiful voice and plays an instrument well, for they hear your words, but do not put them into practice.

The Jews six centuries before Christ had developed an appetite for "preaching as entertainment"—a sort of "massage" theology. "Make us laugh, make us cry, make us sing. But don't you dare make us think or make us change!" They were content to listen and not act.[11] God rebuked them openly for this recreational approach to spirituality. I fear that the American church in the twilight of the twentieth century is not much different. Increasingly, we are the ones who define the terms of discipleship rather than God Himself. We decide which aspects of the Christian faith are suited to our lifestyle and schedule, rather than building our lives around our faith. That is the essence of autonomy. And autonomy, the determination to be independent from the demands of God, is the essence of sin.[12] It is no trifling matter.

The evangelical church in America has become a moral mirror image of the larger culture. We have created the illusion of separateness by developing a religious subculture complete with its own industries. But under inspection, it becomes clear that we are as self-indulging as the larger culture, and nearly as autonomous.

This secularization is a serious deviation from God's plans for His people, and as such constitutes large-scale spiritual decay. This places the next generation at risk more than all the ills of society combined. And as we shall see, the reason they are at risk is a consequence of the age-old way that worldviews are passed from one generation to another.

NOTES

1. John R. W. Stott, *Christian Counter-Culture: The Message of the Sermon on the Mount* (Downers Grove, Ill.: InterVarsity, 1979), p. 19.

2. "A Critical Essay upon the Faculties of the Mind," quoted in *The International Thesaurus of Quotations*, no. 1707 (New York: Harper & Row, 1970), p. 439.

3. Richard Quebedeaux, *The Worldly Evangelicals* (New York: Harper & Row, 1978), p. 13.

4. Stanly Hauerwas and William H. Willimon, *Resident Aliens* (Nashville: Abingdon, 1989), p. 27.

5. Charles Colson, *Kingdoms in Conflict* (Grand Rapids, Mich.: Zondervan/Morrow, 1987), p. 214.

6. Ibid.

7. Oswald Chambers, *My Utmost for His Highest* (Westwood, N.J.: Barbour, n.d.), p. 173.

8. Kirk Kilpatick, interviewed in *His*, December 1984, p. 13.

9. Douglas Groothuis, *Unmasking the New Age* (Downers Grove, Ill.: InterVarsity, 1986), p. 71.

10. The fact that Zondervan, which published MacArthur's book in 1988, would release a response to it (Zane Hodges, *Absolutely Free*) a year later indicates that MacArthur's thesis hit a nerve.

11. See Jeremiah 6:10.

12. See Isaiah 14:13-15; 65:2.

The story of conservative Protestantism in America is in some ways the story of the pilgrim in John Bunyan's epic allegory. . . . Bunyan's pilgrim stumbles into innumerable difficulties and temptations—from the Slough of Despond to Doubting Castle; from the Town of Vanity to the Valley of Humiliation; from Hill Difficulty to the Valley of the Shadow of Death. . . . . Yet, what our pilgrim (evangelicalism) endures and Bunyan's does not is a long and sustained season in the Labyrinths of Modernity. Not only does he emerge a little dizzy and confused, but out of the experience our traveler is transformed. The pilgrim becomes a tourist. Though still headed toward the Celestial Country, he is now traveling with less conviction, less confidence about his path, and is perhaps more vulnerable to the worldly distractions encountered by Bunyan's pilgrim.

James Davison Hunter
Evangelicalism:
The Coming Generation

13

A Chip Off the Old Block

The imprint of the present generation of evangelicals on the rising one was the subject of an extensive study, the Evangelical Academy Project. From 1982 to 1985, University of Virginia sociologist James Davison Hunter conducted an "attitudinal survey of students and faculty at . . . nine Christian liberal arts colleges and seven Evangelical seminaries."[1] The schools Hunter used for his survey were from the "cream" of Christian education in America. "Each of these institutions is committed by charter to maintaining and propagating the core theological and religious tenets of the Evangelical world view," Hunter explains. "This sample of colleges and seminaries represents higher education at the very heart of mainstream American Evangelicalism."[2]

The results of Hunter's survey indicate a noticeably significant shift away from the orthodoxy of the last generation in a number of vital areas: theology, psychology, view of self, and politics.[3] And the shift is in the direction of the larger secular culture.

THEOLOGICAL ACCOMMODATION

The survey revealed a subtle deterioration in views on the Bible, salvation, and evangelism. More than one-half of all surveyed stated that "the Bible is the inspired Word of God," but that "it is not always to be taken literally in its statements concerning matters of science and historical reporting, etc."[4]

While maintaining a conservative view of the Scriptures and their interpretation, the next generation does not believe the traditional emphasis on an inerrant Bible is as significant as did the preceding generation. Apparently they are willing to allow man rather than God to have the final say on the meaning of Scripture.

This tragic error is worsened by the reality of large-scale biblical illiteracy within evangelicalism as a whole. It is one thing to say that God may not have meant certain things recorded in the Bible to be taken in a literal way. The problem comes when the people asserting such a non-literal interpretation lack the desire to acquire the Bible knowledge needed to discuss such matters intelligently. Rather than the next generation simply reaching different scholarly conclusions than those reached by their parents, they are interpreting the Bible in an entirely new way. They force the Bible to conform with their felt needs and desires, rather than subjugating their lives to the demands of Scripture. Although the obvious immediate benefit is a greater personal freedom, the tragic long-range outcome is the eventual loss of any consistent unifying factor for life itself.

The next generation of evangelicals is dismantling the entire basis for a cohesive worldview that is rooted in the Word of God as it has been historically understood. This is a perilous long-range trend, as evangelical patriarch Carl F. H. Henry acknowledges,[5] and it is progressing relatively unnoticed by the larger conservative church, which sees only the gradual liberalizing of behavior that results.

A second aspect of evangelical theology that the next generation disputes is the exclusive nature of the gospel. While 95 percent responded that they believe in a literal place of torment for the unsaved, one-third also implied that "some other form of arrangement is provided for those not exposed to the truths of Christianity."[6] Hunter analyzes the source of their dissent as the outcome of a struggle between the students' intellects and their emotions—with their emotions winning out. He writes: "The sentiment among the coming generation, then, is mixed. It is clear that they know what they 'should' believe but with that they struggle. Intellectually grasping the soteriological demands of orthodox Christianity is one matter; emotionally accepting them is quite another."[7]

A third related facet that weakens theology for the next generation of evangelicals is their motivation for sharing the gospel. Two-thirds of those surveyed said the main reasons they would give someone for becoming a Christian would be either the "sense of meaning and purpose in life" that faith in Christ provided, or the fact that "God has made a difference" in their own life.[8] While it is sublimely true that being rightly related to God provides the deepest personal satisfaction man can experience, it was because of man's sin, not his lack of self-esteem, that Christ died. For many, the idea of talking to a nonbeliever about hell or judgment was seen as arrogant or in poor taste.

There is a direct cause-and-effect relationship between theology and lifestyle. Therefore, if the next generation of evangelicals is willing to bend orthodoxy to fit a new theology that more easily accommodates self and pleasure, it should also be evident in their beliefs about what constitutes moral and immoral behavior. When asked which of several kinds of behaviors were "morally wrong all of the time," their answers indicate a significant migration toward moral laxity.[9] Eight of the behaviors are listed on the next page with their level of disapproval.

	1950s	1960s	1980s
BEHAVIOR			
Attending "R" rated movies	n/a	n/a	7%
Use of tobacco products	93%	70%	51
Use of alcohol products	98	78	17
Smoking marijuana	n/a	99	70
Casual "petting"	n/a	48	23
Heavy "petting"	n/a	81	45
Premarital sexual intercourse	n/a	94	89
Extramarital sexual intercourse	n/a	98	97

n/a = not available

The only behaviors that appear to have maintained a high level of disapproval between the two generations involve sexual intercourse. Yet, the recent data released by Christian researchers on teen sexuality indicate that, while evangelical young people may believe sex outside of marriage is sinful, their theology is having little impact on their sexual habits.[10] Christian young people, like their nonbelieving counterparts, are succumbing to sexual pressure at an alarming rate.

Are Christians More Selfish Than Non-Christians?

Youth historically has been noted for its idealistic altruism. Is that still the case? Let's compare four responses of evangelical college students, seminarians, and public university students to statements about the self.[11]

The next generation of evangelicals is as concerned about the self as their secular counterparts. However, the most sobering truth in these figures comes in the last two statements: apparently a larger number of nonbelievers perceive Christianity as existing primarily for the benefit of others than do the next generation of Christians themselves! The implications of this are staggering. If the watching world expects to see conservative Christians oriented outwardly, only to discover that they are as inwardly focused as the larger

STATEMENT	PERCENT AGREEING		
	Evangelical College Students	Seminarians	Public University Students
Self improvement is important to me and I work hard at it.	87%	82%	87%
I feel a strong need for new experiences.	68	52	78
A good Christian will strive to be a "well-rounded person."	79	80	48
For the Christian, realizing your full potential as a human being is just as important as putting others before you.	62	46	44

culture, the truth of the gospel is reduced to merely an apparent difference in lifestyle preference rather than an issue of one's eternal destiny. Faith is then understood merely as a matter of personal choice rather than as alignment with eternal truth.

Hunter documents that the self-obsession evident among the students in his study is true of the larger evangelical population as well.[12] He makes an assertion that is crucial to understand. He states that the obsession with self is understood by evangelicals as a truly biblical and therefore valid preoccupation:

> The self and human subjectivity have not only gained attention but have gained legitimacy as well. They have attained a positive value in Evangelical culture. Logically, any discussion of self-improvement, self-fulfillment, and "self-actualization" presupposes that the self can be and is worth be-

ing improved, fulfilled, and actualized; any discussion of human potentiality and emotional and psychological maturity presupposes these as legitimate and worthwhile goals. Indeed, the self would seem to achieve ultimate significance and ultimate value when these concerns are framed within biblical and Christian symbolism.[13]

The next generation of evangelicals has followed in the footsteps of the parent generation, who regard the self as important. But the next generation has gone a step beyond; they actually believe the self can be legitimately and best embellished within the framework of conservative Christianity. They seem unaware that this understanding of what constitutes conservative Christianity has been largely shaped by a culture in rebellion against God.

SOCIAL SANCTIFICATION

Hunter's study revealed another shift worth noting: change in the understanding of the basic purpose of Christianity. Traditionally, evangelicalism believed that the primary mission of the church was to enlarge the kingdom of God through world evangelization. Saving the lost was the cause to which all were called. Not so with the next generation. They appear to have elevated issues of social justice to a position of importance equal to world evangelization. More than one-half of college students and seminarians considered the pursuit of justice "just as important" or "almost as important" as evangelism.[14]

Social ministry has gained the status of unequivocal Christian responsibility. Many in the next generation assume that those who claim to be genuine Christians will be involved in the issues that concern and threaten society at large. This represents a drastic transformation from the view traditionally held by evangelicalism, that the church's primary function was to bring people into the kingdom of God through personal faith in the atoning work of Jesus Christ.

To be sure, modern evangelicalism has not had a reputation for having much of a remedial impact on society. Men such as Charles Colson, Tony Campolo, Ron Sider, and others committed to the plight of the oppressed have had difficulty raising the collective social conscience of evangelicalism. The idea of social justice is foreign to most adult evangelicals. The tragedy is that the coming generation's increasing motivation for social involvement must be understood against the larger backdrop of their diminishing confidence in the inerrancy of Scripture, their unwillingness to profess the exclusive nature of the gospel, and their belief that self-improvement is part of God's agenda for human history. With the possibility of significant doctrinal deterioration in view, it is likely that the coming generation's orientation will continue to shift away from evangelism to activism.

In the coming decade, involvement and allegiance to social causes will likely become the mistaken touchstone of spirituality. To fight the growing multitude of social diseases in our country seems noble and has the appearance of genuine spirituality. But the truth is their involvement will be motivated merely by a sense of societal obligation rather than by an intimate and dynamic relationship with the God who created, and cares so very much for, those in need. I am not impressed by a generation that is interested in the homeless, the unborn, and the poor, and at the same time is drifting further and further from the eternal absolutes that demand the very lifestyle they espouse. In fact, I am frightened.

Hunter attributes this growing spiritual anemia to a failure within evangelical higher education. But there are other "teachers" who are much more to blame.

NOTES

1. James Davison Hunter, *Evangelicalism: The Coming Generation* (Chicago: U. of Chicago, 1987), p. 9. Hunter's data came from Wheaton College, Gordon College, Westmont College, Taylor University, Messiah College, George Fox College, Bethel College, Seattle Pacific University, and Houghton College. Additional information came from Fuller Theological Seminary, Gordon-Conwell Theological Seminary, Westminster Theological Seminary, Talbot Theological Seminary, Wheaton Graduate School, Asbury Theological Seminary, and Conservative Baptist Theological Seminary (i.e., Denver Seminary).

2. Ibid. Hunter's study has been criticized by some for not containing adequate representation from minorities or charismatic schools. He refutes that assertion on the grounds that the future leadership for evangelicalism will come from the schools he surveyed; therefore, he believes his conclusions are valid.

3. "Passing It On: Will Our Kids Recognize Our Faith?" *World*, March 11, 1989, pp. 5-7.

4. Hunter, *Evangelicalism*, p. 25.

5. "Passing It On," p. 6.

6. Hunter, *Evangelicalism*, p. 35.

7. Ibid., p. 39.

8. Ibid., p. 40.

9. Ibid., p. 59.

10. See Josh McDowell and Dick Day, *Why Wait?* (San Bernardino, Calif.: Here's Life, 1987).

11. Hunter, Evangelicalism, p. 66.

12. Ibid., pp. 68-69.

13. Ibid., p. 69.

14. Ibid., p. 43.

Children have never been very good at listening to their elders, but they have never failed to imitate them.

James Baldwin
Nobody Knows My Name

A student is not above his teacher, but everyone who is fully trained will be like his teacher.

Jesus Christ
Luke 6:40

14

LIKE SHEPHERD, LIKE SHEEP

Educators often refer to the "formal" and "informal" curricula as the two primary channels of instruction and learning. The majority of what is traditionally understood as education is built around the formal curriculum. It is the structured part of education: lesson plans, lectures, exams, and the like. Its essential medium is the spoken word, and its primary concern is the dissemination of information.

The informal curriculum, on the other hand, is not planned. It is spontaneous rather than structured, seen rather than heard, and often learned more subconsciously than consciously. Whereas the formal curriculum is what teachers teach, the informal curriculum is how teachers live. One has to do with the distribution of data, the other with the formulation of values. One is learned from a text, the other from a lifestyle. Jesus was well acquainted with this distinction:

> Then Jesus said to the crowds and to his disciples: "The teachers of the law and the Pharisees sit in Moses' seat. So you must obey them and do everything they tell you [formal curriculum]. But do not do what they do [informal curriculum], for they do not practice what they preach." (Matthew 23:1-3)

157

> A student is not above his teacher, but everyone who is fully
> trained [formal] will be like his teacher [informal]. (Luke
> 6:40)

We have a natural tendency to imitate those in positions
of authority in our lives. But the teachers with the most significant and lasting impact on the next generation of evangelicals are not in the classrooms of Christian universities or
even Christian high schools. They are in the kitchens and living rooms of evangelical homes.

From the beginning, God knew that the spirituality of
children would be the fruit of their natural spiritual curios-
ity encountering the lifestyles of their parents. "In the future, when your son asks you, 'What is the meaning of the
stipulations, decrees and laws the Lord our God has com-
manded you?' tell him . . ." Moses said (Deuteronomy 6:20).
God told His people that the day would arrive in each of
their families when their children would want an answer for
the reasons behind their faith. Moses told the Israelites to
make sure they had something to tell them. The answer was
not supposed to be merely a "creed." It was to emerge from a
deep personal trust in the God of Israel. Their answer should
be linked to their personal lives, not simply to a national
theology:

> Hear, O Israel: The Lord our God, the Lord is one. Love the
> Lord your God with all your heart and with all your soul and
> with all your strength. These commandments that I give you
> today are to be upon your hearts. Impress them on your chil-
> dren. Talk about them when you sit at home and when you
> walk along the road, when you lie down and when you get up.
> Tie them as symbols on your hands and bind them on your
> foreheads. Write them on the doorframes of your houses and
> on your gates. (Deuteronomy 6:4-8)

God instructed His people to teach their children this
way because it is how children learn. Tragically, this essential insight about the transferral of spiritual life and truth

from one generation to another has been nearly lost in our day. The tiny remnant that exists has degenerated into an industry. Christian bookstores are sated with Scripture-quoting plaques, pins, buttons, and bumper stickers—the twentieth-century vestige of God's mandate in Deuteronomy 6.

It is possible for parents to have the name of Jesus plastered all over their home, checks, clothing, and vehicles yet have little of the character and values of Christ in their lives. The result is a sort of spiritual schizophrenia—a polarized faith that consists of a verbal affirmation of the truths of historic Christianity by means of things like family devotions, Sunday school, and youth group (formal curriculum), and the simultaneous denial of those same truths in lifestyle (informal curriculum). Because the informal curriculum has a more abiding influence than the formal curriculum, the children develop their theology, values, and subsequent lifestyle from what they see instead of what they hear. We can see the outcomes in several key areas.

RESPECT FOR AUTHORITY

Consider respect for authority. Like a birthmark, it's a key distinctive among evangelical Christians. Thousands have attended large-scale seminars dedicated to teaching the place of authority in the Christian's life. The leaders argue that God places various authority figures in our lives while growing up because He ultimately wants us to learn to obey Him. It is extremely difficult, perhaps impossible, for someone to obey God, whom they have never seen, if they are unwilling to obey visible and tangible human authorities. We instill this into our children's minds from an early age with fervor and regularity. Christian young people hear it at home, in Sunday school, at church, in youth groups, at church camps, and in the Christian day schools. If we could devise a way to get it into their food and water, I think we would!

When it comes to the formal curriculum on the principle of authority, we've got every base covered. But what about the informal curriculum—the real pedagogue in our home? What are our children really learning about authority?

While directing traffic after school each day, I have seen hundreds of parents arrive to pick up their children. Several cars have a conspicuous piece of gadgetry on the dashboard that teaches a lesson on authority contrary to everything I have tried to instill in my classroom through both subject matter and personal example. I suspect that it also contradicts the formal curriculum of the home that housed the car.

A radar detector may seem like an innocuous piece of circuitry and plastic, but it is actually a powerful informal instructor about the principle of authority. Similarly, I often see cars sporting Christian bumper stickers speed past me so fast I can't even read their "witness for Christ" until I catch up to them at the next stoplight. Yet, it doesn't occur to most adults that the trip to school in the morning has the potential of negating what was learned earlier that morning at family devotions. What we say about authority has no lasting impact if it is not supported by a congruent lifestyle. What were the children in these particular homes really being taught about obedience to authority? They were learning that:

- The goal of obedience is to not get caught.
- The purpose of obedience is to avoid punishment.
- Obedience is arbitrary. (I decide what is worth obeying.)
- Some dishonesty is OK.

How we talk about our employers, pastors, and neighbors in front of our children determines how they perceive our own convictions about respect for authority.

A young man boasted that his father, a prominent leader in a large evangelical organization, was going to disconnect the catalytic converter on their new car as soon as the warranty expired so he could burn leaded gas. That young man could have recited a long list of Bible verses about authority, based on his father's careful instruction. But you can guess which principle actually guided his daily actions. He was dishonest and deceitful, and to this day his father cannot understand why.

THE SOVEREIGNTY OF GOD

We all want our children to grow up believing "God loves them and has a wonderful plan for their lives." We want them to learn to trust God. We take pains to tell them that God can be trusted and that He always "works everything together for good." We lecture them about trust when their lives seem to be falling apart. But how do we respond to life on a fallen planet? A lost job? A missed promotion? The theft of our possessions? Do our children see us struggle and fight for our "rights," or do they witness genuine pain followed by submission to the will of the God who works everything together for good? Do our children believe that God is bigger than an incompetent official at a crucial basketball game, or have our actions taught them that He can only be trusted for "spiritual" things?

As with respect for authority, our children will develop their understanding of God's sovereignty from our lives, not from our mouths. This principle applies equally to what they come to truly believe about prayer, suffering, forgiveness, love, and the host of other doctrines of evangelical Christianity.

THE CENTRALITY OF THE HOME

For the evangelical, the home is the supposed center of all meaningful life and the citadel of all that is true and good. We verbally agree that its demise will certainly guarantee the eventual collapse of Western culture. We attack with a vengeance any institution or individual accused of trying to destroy the family or traditional values. James Dobson, host of the radio program "Focus on the Family," can virtually guarantee that more than one hundred thousand letters of concern will be sent anywhere he directs, by his suggesting that the home or traditional values are under attack by the person or agency in question.

We provide the illusion of pit-bull tenacity when it comes to our commitment to the home. Evangelical church pulpits reverberate with homilies on the home, and evangelical publishers churn out books about marriage and family. Clearly we are *telling* the world that our homes are an inviolable sanctuary; a shrine to all we hold dear. But what is the actual message we *show* our children concerning the sanctity of marriage and family, or about the centrality of the home?

They see widespread divorce among Christians. A casual pass through the religion section of your local newspaper will quickly reveal that divorce recovery workshops, step-parenting clinics, and singles ministries characterize the weekly fare for many congregations. The eighties was a decade when most churches had to redefine their ministries and, sadly for some, their theologies. The next generation of Christians may be hearing a great deal about the sanctity of marriage, but they aren't seeing much evidence.

To acknowledge that divorce and remarriage exist in the church and then seek to minister to its casualties is one thing. But to present it to the next generation as an evangelical option is quite another. The time has come for the evangelical church in America to make a clear statement to itself and the next generation regarding God's standard for marriage and family. And the most effective platform from which to herald such a message is the dinner tables and family rooms in individual homes within the church.

The next generation continually hears and reads that traditional family values are under attack. Magazines like Focus on the Family's *Citizen* report the present attempts of government, media, and private interest groups to undermine traditional values and the family; their ministries are helpful, indeed essential. However, I am beginning to wonder where all the traditional families are. Most mothers I know work outside the home. More and more churches are offering day-care services. Growing numbers of couples are choosing to limit families or remain childless. Many of my students' families rarely eat more than a couple of meals together during an entire week. An increasing number of "nuclear" families in our school consist of two divorced adults who have remarried and brought children from each of the previous marriages into the new family. My own classrooms contain one or two more children each year whose parents have decided to call it "quits." One freshman boy actually splits up each month's living accommodations between two sets of parents in the same city.

Many of these new family arrangements are legitimate, of course. However, the present generation cannot speak glibly of traditional family values within a context that is rapidly becoming nontraditional. When we do so we surely confuse the next generation about the biblical standard in these areas.

These informal instructors are molding the theology of the future church. The formal message our young people are hearing contradicts the truths they are seeing in the corporate life of the church. We are perplexed, frustrated, even angry that our children seem to be abandoning the faith they were "taught." But the sobering truth is that they are merely being more honest with what they have actually learned from us, their teachers.

This is not an attempt to blame Christian parents for their children's problems. What our children become is ultimately the result of their own choices. But we must not ignore the obvious truth that as teachers we have often become a moral mirror image of a self-absorbed and morally bankrupt culture. When the sixties collapsed, American culture began to die. That illness is now at our doorsteps. The children in our homes are the generation at risk. And they are also the hope of the church. But the responsibility for reclaiming this generation at risk falls squarely upon us, the generation that helped put them there.

Part 4

CAN THE FOUNDATIONS
BE RESTORED?

The book of Daniel tells us that Nebuchadnezzar failed in his attempt to turn Daniel, Shadrach, Meshach and Abednego, but we can assume that many other Israelite youths were turned into idol worshippers. That's the way it always is: a battle of worldviews, with the next generation as the prize.

Herbert Schlossberg
and Marvin Olasky,
*Turning Point: A Christian
Worldview Declaration*

15

A BIBLICAL WORLDVIEW

In working intimately with a large number of evangelical high school students and their parents over the past few years, I have faced a startling paradox. The number of my students who brazenly espouse secular values grows larger, while the number who appear to be interested in knowing and pleasing God continues to diminish.

More and more students each year are becoming sexually active. I can expect at least one student per semester to drop out of school due to pregnancy. Besides the obvious shifts in behavior, attitudes are also changing. Disrespect and dishonesty are still viewed as inappropriate—but no longer serious. Some within the faculty have even left the teaching profession because they could no longer tolerate the insolence. Even the school superintendent and principals find themselves confronted with increasing hostility and indignation—from parents! I recently witnessed a sophomore boy ridicule his mother in my presence. When I told him my mother would have knocked me across the room for a comment like his, his mother looked at me, surprised I would say such a thing!

Students in our Christian school display a diminishing sense of loyalty and ownership, while the number of those who envy the flagrant sin of many in the public school is rising. This visible shift in values and behavior is not restricted to the students, as though our school is the corrupting culprit. The homes are exhibiting adult versions of similar ungodly behavior: adultery, abuse, divorce, and a host of other manifestations of self-centeredness.

Because I am acquainted with the biblical doctrines of original sin and man's depravity, this spiritual decay does not totally surprise me. The Bible clearly teaches that things will get worse before they get better, and that the corruption of God's people by the surrounding culture is a perennial problem. What amazes me is the response to these behaviors on the part of many engaging in them. There is no lasting regret, no feelings of guilt, no inner conflict. There is always some initial pain and remorse, but it quickly evaporates. Somehow, many of my students are able to live a dual life. Their Christian faith has become little more than a spiritual version of a bilingual dictionary, something to be pulled out only when circumstances demand it.

Some of you may feel the explanation is obvious: They aren't really Christians at all! I am sure that is the case for some. But it doesn't adequately explain the phenomenon I am witnessing. There is ample evidence of spiritual vitality in many of my students' lives. Simply assigning them to the realm of unbelief is convenient but inadequate. There is something much deeper that allows them to live with multiple spiritual personalities—each with a separate conscience.

Herbert Schlossberg and Marvin Olasky's book *Turning Point: A Christian Worldview Declaration*[1] provided me with an interpretive framework in which to make sense of what I was seeing and experiencing. Although our school was doing an outstanding job of providing a Bible curriculum that was relevant, thoughtful, and sound, we were deficient in an essential ingredient of true discipleship: We were not teaching our students how to "think Christianly." While teaching Bible surveys, apologetics, humanitarian skills, principles of daily discipleship, and a biblical view of marriage and family, we were not helping them see how it all fits together. It is much like trying to teach human anatomy with only a box full of bones but no intact skeleton. Or like having all the pieces to a jigsaw puzzle but not the box with the picture. In short, they were not being helped to develop a uniquely Christian worldview.[2]

My students were accumulating information about God, man, and the Bible, but had no way to connect it all. Because their faith had been reduced to the mere amassing of facts and behavioral lists, they missed the more sobering realization that biblical truth is inherently moral truth. It has authority over every aspect of life simply by virtue of its source—God Himself. Schlossberg and Olasky contend that any Christian education that gives students facts without vision has failed.[3]

I was witnessing the fruit of that failure each day. But Schlossberg and Olasky's indictment is even more appropriate for the Christian home than for the church or the Christian day school. Children pick up their vision from the informal curriculum in their lives. While it is certainly true that worldviews can be polished and fine-tuned by the church and the Christian day school, the larger truth is that for young people, worldviews are assembled in the home. Parents, not the school, are ultimately responsible for molding their child's outlook.

Nonetheless, as a teacher of a Christian day school, I completely rewrote my senior Bible curriculum to focus on the principle of worldview. One week was spent on each of ten key questions about life from the standpoint of both secular and biblical worldviews. We sought answers in the Bible for the problems that any worldview, whether Christian or secular, must address and answer to be legitimate. The ten issues of life we discussed were:[4]

- *Individuality:* Who or what am I?
- *Meaning:* What's the point of it all?
- *Values:* How am I to make moral choices?
- *Truth:* Is it possible to know the truth about ourselves and the universe?
- *Love:* What is love, and where can it be found?
- *Suffering:* Why is there suffering, and how can we live with it?
- *Death:* How am I to face death? Is there life after death?
- *Hope:* What hope is there for the human race?
- *Reality:* Is there anything more than the physical world?
- *Evil:* Is there any hope in fighting evil and injustice?

A number of curious things began to happen as we examined secular and biblical answers to the above ten questions. Those who were intently following what we were doing gradually began to see that biblical Christianity made sense of life as it really is. They slowly realized that being a Christian was not just a matter of saying yes to a creed. It involved all of life and demanded the alignment of their lives with God's will.

In discussing the biblical answer to the question of individuality, they discovered that their individuality is a product of God's intimate involvement in their own personal origin (Psalm 139). They also realized that human beings have personality because they are made in the image and likeness of a personal God (Genesis 1:27). The most important discovery they made was that only the Judeo-Christian worldview provides mankind with a valid basis for human dignity. Because man is the image-bearer of God, he is distinct from the rest of creation (Genesis 9:6). For example, they saw that there is a biblical explanation for why, when someone sees a small boy and his dog about to be hit by a car, they will always try to save the child first.

We then discussed the implications of this principle in various social and political arenas, such as abortion, capital punishment, the plight of the homeless, Third-World oppression, and racism. They quickly understood that a distinctly biblical worldview affects their perspective on everything that has to do with people, because all people have dignity by virtue of their creation.

High school students love to discuss things that are too distant to create discomfort. So I brought the issue home, in the truest sense of the word. I asked if the image of God in man should have any impact on other areas or relationships in our lives. Slowly, for some, the lights came on. One student said, "Shouldn't it affect the way we treat people in general? I mean like waitresses and clerks in stores?" Soon we were discussing how a biblical worldview should impact the way we treat people everywhere, all the time, whether it's on the highway or on the phone. And taking it a step further, they saw that the image of God in man demanded that they treat their parents and siblings with dignity too.

All this and more came from serious study of only one small facet of a biblical worldview. Once they began to understand their faith in terms of a comprehensive worldview, the implications for their own behavior and outlook became obvious. Suddenly, being a Christian was much more than simply saying yes to a cluster of theological doctrines. It was life—their life. All of it, all of the time.

Another unexpected thing also happened. Many of my students experienced a revitalized confidence in the authority of the Bible and a desire to better understand it. They gradually began to comprehend the significance of the evangelical doctrine that the Bible is the Word of God, and that it is therefore true, authoritative, and trustworthy. One of the primary causes for the rampant spread of biblical illiteracy among Christians (especially youth)[5] is that we no longer believe the Bible can speak relevantly, much less authoritatively, in an age of technological and relational complexity. When students began to understand that it does so speak, they also felt a need to know and understand the Scriptures better.

Of course, understanding the concept of a biblical worldview and helping young people try to develop one didn't turn all of them into bionic believers. The lost principle of a biblical worldview is no panacea for a generation that is under siege. But it did help them better understand what a genuine Christian is, and, even more significantly, it helped them understand their own relationship to God. Even those who upon graduation abandoned their professed faith for life in the fast lane at least understood more completely the seriousness of their choices.

The most solid preventive action we can take to protect and preserve the next generation is to help them develop a biblical worldview when they are children. But in order to pass on a worldview that is distinctly biblical, we obviously must first possess one ourselves. Do we? Or is worldview perhaps the neglected essential component of adult spirituality too?

A close friend who ministers to Christian businessmen in our city recently confided that he has seen a common syndrome in the lives of most of the men he is working with. According to him, "They lack a unifying factor for all of life." These businessmen perceive their relationship with God merely as one among many facets of their personal and professional lives that need to be kept in balance. They do not have a comprehensive outlook, stemming from their relationship with God, that becomes the unifying factor for all of life. Christianity is merely a piece of their lives, not the whole. Consequently, they think and act in terms of priorities instead of worldview.

This at least partially explains why someone can have a sullied reputation in the business community and still be a celebrity in the church. Or how a man can leave his wife and family for another woman in the church, yet still believe he can be a faithful Christian. The central reason more and more Christians' lives are unraveling faster than they can be repaired is because there is no unifying factor to their faith, only a prescribed creed and a list of behaviors. Unless their faith in Jesus Christ yields a comprehensive biblical worldview, it will be blown apart by the winds of adversity and passion.

But why do people need to be conscious of the principle of worldview? Why do Christians in particular need to be so serious about developing a distinctly biblical worldview? Or more important, what exactly is a biblical worldview and where and how does a Christian cultivate one? Our ability to reclaim the generation at risk will depend largely upon our answers to these three questions.

NOTES

1. Herbert Schlossberg and Marvin Olasky, *Turning Point: A Christian Worldview Declaration* (Westchester, Ill.: Crossway, 1987).

2. Francis Schaeffer's books *Death in the City, The Church at the End of the Twentieth Century, The Mark of the Christian*, and *The Christian Manifesto* all urged the people of God to bring the lordship of Jesus Christ into all areas of their lives, which is essentially the principle of worldview. Schaeffer was one of the first evangelicals who strove to present a comprehensive understanding of Christianity. In the late sixties, he was sharply criticized for being too philosophical. In the late seventies, he was criticized for being too simplistic. Finally, after two decades of preaching to predominantly deaf ears, Schaeffer became more radical in his orientation toward cultural evil and the believer's responsibility to abet it. He was then too radical for many within evangelicalism. He tirelessly proclaimed the truth of God to a church that applauded the depth of his teaching yet failed to heed its message.

3. Schlossberg and Olasky, *Turning Point*, p. 35.

4. The ten "key questions" appear in and are developed from Colin Chapman, *The Case for Christianity* (Grand Rapids, Mich.: Eerdmans, 1981).

5. See "Christian Kids Don't Know the Basics," *Group* (September 1989), pp. 51-52. The results of this survey revealed that "overall, Christian teenagers spend more time praying than reading the Bible."

A Biblical worldview gives us a clear look at reality. When we move away from that clear view, we are like children increasingly smudging a window with dirty fingerprints and then looking outside. First the colors become duller. Then the shapes begin to alter. As the dirt gets thicker, the light is progressively shut out. It becomes harder to say with accuracy what is happening out there. If this process takes place gradually, we might hardly notice what is happening, but increasingly we are cut off from reality. . . . To the extent that our worldview departs from God's message to us, our perceptions are distorted.

Herbert Schlossberg
and Marvin Olasky,
*Turning Point: A Christian
Worldview Declaration*

16

FOUNDATIONS OF A BIBLICAL WORLDVIEW

To fully understand the importance of Christians having a distinctly biblical worldview, we need to understand what a worldview is and how it functions. James Sire explains the necessity for a worldview this way:

> The world flings itself at us in a constant barrage of data—the data of our five senses, the messages of ordinary conversations, of traffic signals, of billboards and books, of radio and television. Our mental and spiritual health depends on having a frame of reference that can sort out the useful from the useless, the meaningful from the meaningless, the trivial from the profound. The problem is this: when a new idea comes our way, what are we going to do with it? How will we identify and label it so that we can make it a congenital part of our mental furniture?[1]

But a worldview is infinitely more than just a mental sentry. It is also the essential interpreter of life's meaning for each of us. "Like a pair of colored sunglasses, a worldview colors the way we interpret the events around us."[2] Everyone has a worldview; no one is exempt—even those who are ignorant of philosophy and theology. And we are constantly inundated with the worldviews of those around us, especially of

those who are the "molders and shapers" of American culture—those involved in education and in the broadcast and
entertainment media. Our worldviews intersect, overlap, and
conflict with one another. Unfortunately, most secular education and media present a distinctly anti-Christian worldview. TV czar Ted Turner is anything but clandestine about
his own feelings toward biblical faith: "Christianity is a religion for losers. I don't want anybody to die for me. I've had a
few drinks and a few girlfriends, and if that's gonna put me
in hell, then so be it."[3]

These are not merely the comments of a man with poor
taste. Ted Turner has a comprehensive worldview just like
everyone else. Only his is contradictory to almost everything
Christians embrace. And he is not passive about his worldview, either. It is both naive and foolish to assume that Turner's
anti-Christian bias is not reflected in the programming on
his networks.

Schlossberg and Olasky maintain that while education
and the communications media boast that they provide a
marketplace for ideas, they are actually battlefields for dif-
fering worldviews.[4] The leaders of these enterprises have
chosen which side they are on; they have a distinct agenda,
and they are inflicting heavy casualties among unsuspecting
evangelicals who naively assume they are merely being entertained. Ignorance of this fact creates the distinct possibility that a secular worldview may gradually become that of
the evangelical viewer or listener.

Our worldview interprets data, but it also dictates our
choices. This is as true for "objective" scientists as it is for
subjective philosophers. Noted astronomer Carl Sagan, for
example, has said, "The Cosmos is all that is or ever was or
ever will be."[5] He did not arrive at these atheistic convictions from protracted time spent looking into space. He
brought those convictions to the study of the stars. Consequently, where a Christian astronomer sees increasing evidence of design and order in the heavens and is affirmed in

his faith in an intelligent Designer, Sagan sees the growth of his understanding of this same evidence as an indication of his decreasing need for God. Two intelligent men examine the same data and arrive at opposing conclusions, all because of the influence of their respective worldviews.

Jesus Christ knew the critical importance of worldview. His statements to his followers about listening and seeing were centered around *how* more than *what* they looked at and listened to:

> Therefore consider carefully how you listen. Whoever has will be given more; whoever does not have, even what he thinks he has will be taken from him. (Luke 8:18)

> The eye is the lamp of the body. If your eyes are good, your whole body will be full of light. But if your eyes are bad, your whole body will be full of darkness. If then the light within you is darkness, how great is that darkness! (Matthew 6:22-23)

Unfortunately, as Christians most of us have settled for mere concern about what we watch and listen to. We have established a host of unwritten lists of acceptable and unacceptable Christian behavior—the evangelical equivalent of the mortal and venial sins of Catholicism.

These lists differ from family to family. This often happens with Christian parents trying to set guidelines for their children regarding rock music. Instead of the parents helping the child learn to discern what it is that's wrong with a particular group or song, he is simply told not to listen to it. The parents of one of my students actually drove two screws into their son's radio dial to prevent him from tuning in offensive stations. He's long since left his home and his faith in God, but not his music.

Of course, I am not advocating the open acceptance of R-rated films and sexually explicit music. But blind prohibitions or endorsements of certain behaviors is not the answer either. While providing the temporary illusion of spiritual maturity, this approach ignores the more critical need to be able to discern what is right or wrong about something. Such discernment is the product of a well-developed worldview, not a list of behaviors learned by rote and reinforced through reward and punishment.

THE WORLDVIEW PROCESS

The best evidence of one's worldview is his lifestyle. A secular worldview will yield a secular lifestyle even if it is clothed in the robes of Christian jargon. Our worldview dictates how we perceive life. It influences our hierarchy of values—what is important to us. We decide those things that are important to us; then we set the "wheel" of our lives in motion in order to achieve those things. Then, as the wheel begins to roll, our lifestyle (the rim) makes contact with the people in our lives, while our worldview (the hub) remains relatively hidden from their scrutiny. (See illustration below.)

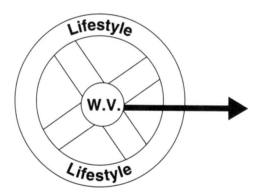

Unfortunately, for most Americans and growing numbers of evangelical Christians, this process is reversed. People now decide how they wish to live first. Once that is established, they adopt the values of that lifestyle. Their final step is to formulate a worldview, often complete with a contrived or compromised deity, that supports and encourages their self-derived values and lifestyle. Nothing could be more simple . . . or more devastating. Those of us in the church see the glaring flaws of a "secular theology," where man creates a god in his own image and likeness. We are quick to believe that we are immune from this malady simply because we are Christians.

Because most Christians are ignorant of the principle of worldview, they consciously or unconsciously separate the various areas of their lives. These "compartments" are isolated and insulated from one another and therefore do not impinge on each other. On paper it tends to look like the illustration below:

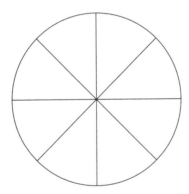

In the process of slicing up our life like a pie, we have reduced Christian faith to mere faithfulness in the spiritual slice. We have come to believe that if we are faithful to give to God what "belongs" to Him—Sunday morning, some effort at prayer and Bible reading, 10 percent of our income— then He has no business poking around in the other areas of our lives. In fact, we actually seem to believe that God is not even interested in those areas, just as long as we are "good." For many evangelicals, morality has become the modern measure of spirituality. Goodness is the twentieth-century equivalent of godliness.

MBAs, BMWs, and "EXCELLENCE"

This viewpoint was perennially expressed by my seniors. Every year I had them write a two-page paper on "What I Want to Do with My Life and Why." I stored their work and mailed it to them one year later. Reading their papers was enlightening. One young man from a solid evangelical home wrote, "I want to attend a private college, secure an MBA, a BMW and a condo in Vail. I realize that these are not very noble goals, but it's what I want to do with my life." His honesty is to be commended. But the larger tragedy is that this future evangelical adult's values and goals are no different from those of the kid down the street who wants nothing to do with Jesus Christ.

How did the young man reconcile this apparent conflict in values? He said that he would be faithful to God through "honesty" and "excellence." He actually believed that being a moral person enabled him to espouse the same values, aim for the same goals, and live for the same reasons as his non-believing peers. There was no mention of God, personal sacrifice, or investment in the lives of people. And there was certainly no conflict in this boy's heart regarding his visions for himself. His "spirituality" was comfortably insulated in its own little compartment where it would not upset, much less infect, the other areas of his life.

He saw no connection between his relationship with God and his professional goals. The purposes of God for human history were understood only in terms of his private success. The result of this compartmentalized, schizophrenic spirituality is a *secular worldview encrusted in a sacred vocabulary.* That phrase describes more and more evangelical Christians.[6] Being ignorant of the principle of worldview results in the compartmentalization and confinement of our faith.

Our ignorance also makes us unguarded about the opposing, even hostile, worldviews around us. With a compartmentalized faith, a sacred vocabulary, and a false sense of spirituality, we eventually assume we have a Christian world-view simply because we are Christians. This pallid reasoning makes us easy prey for those wishing to reform our world-view, such as secular educators and the media.

Another factor enhances the society's secularizing influ-ence on our worldview: The impact of sin affects man's abili-ty to trust the conclusions of his intellect. Apart from revela-tion from God, man's depravity naturally leads his unaided reasoning away from biblical truth.

The potential for distortion of truth grows as principles and disciplines move from the concrete toward the abstract. (See illustration on next page.) Without an external standard by which to compare his thoughts and conclusions, man be-comes the final judge of what is true. And if man becomes the source of truth, then his conclusions on how to live be-come absolute also. But then, who decides who's "truth" is actually "true"?

This is precisely the dilemma modern secular education finds itself in. With no source of absolutes, the search for a basis for ethics and values is futile.

Christians without a solid biblical worldview will often become confused in an environment where they are con-stantly exposed to the worldviews of the secular culture. It is no wonder that many Christian young people return from college as professing agnostics. Without a firm foundation, their worldview will become identical to that of the nonbe-lieving world by default. They may assume their worldview is still Christian because they retain their sacred vocabulary and some religious customs. This process of "conversion" to a secular worldview often takes place even among students at evangelical colleges and seminaries. If they assume a pro-fessor holds a biblical worldview simply because he is a Christian, they may accept what he teaches as "the gospel truth," even though his viewpoint is more secular than Christian.

The principle of worldview is crucial. A distinctly bibli-cal worldview is conspicuously absent from the lives of the majority of American evangelicals, young and old. Recapturing a sense of its necessity and reinforcing our own biblical worldview may be our most vital task in the twilight of the twentieth century. This is critical, not merely for our own spiritual health, but also for that of the next generation. But, before we can begin to see all of life through the window of a biblical worldview, we will have to thoroughly clean the glass, for I am convinced that it has become seriously smudged.

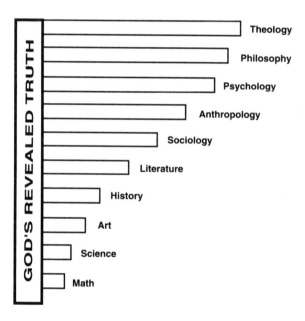

Potential for Distortion In Knowledge

Notes

1. James Sire, *Scripture Twisting* (Downers Grove, Ill.: InterVarsity, 1980), p. 25.
2. "Understanding World Views," *Common Ground*, August 1988.
3. Quoted in *World*, November 11, 1989, p. 4.
4. Herbert Schlossberg and Marvin Olasky, *Turning Point: A Christian Worldview Declaration* (Westchester, Ill.: Crossway, 1987), p. 71.
5. Carl Sagan, *Cosmos* (New York: Random, 1980), p. 4.
6. Another particularly enlightening assignment involved "values clarification." I took a standard secular values clarification exercise and made one small change to it. After the students listed their top ten values and validated them, I asked them to find explicit or implicit support for their values from the Bible. In other words, I asked them to show me where God valued the same things they did. I'll never forget one distraught senior girl who came up to me during class and moaned, "Mr. Sciacca, I've done this entire assignment, but I can't find a single passage of Scripture to support what's important to me!" She was upset with the Bible for not containing the verses she needed!

Augustine's view of the relation of the Christian to culture is most clearly expressed in his work The City of God. . . . *The two cities are the city of God and the city of man. . . . These two societies, though already present with Adam himself, emerge specifically in Cain and Abel. "Cain founded a city, whereas Abel, as a pilgrim, did not found one," says Augustine. "For the city of saints is up above, although it produces citizens here below, and in their persons the city is on pilgrimage until the time of its Kingdom comes." For this reason the one city is rooted in "worldly possession" and the other in "heavenly hopes."*

Robert Webber
The Secular Saint

17

EVANGELICALS: NATIVES, ALIENS, OR TOURISTS?

To know what a distinctively biblical worldview is, why it is so vital, and how to cultivate one are essential prerequisites to reclaiming the rising generation of Christian youth —a generation that is indeed at risk. But I am convinced that even this will prove to be futile unless it is preceded by a purifying "baptism of fire" on what I call our "essential perspective."

While our worldview is the comprehensive way we "see" all of life, our essential perspective is the way you and I "see" ourselves in relation to the world around us and to God Himself. "Essential perspective" is not merely another catchy phrase for the ubiquitous notion of self-esteem. Unfortunately, we have been virtually buried alive by books over the past decade on why it is "biblical" to love ourselves and how to go about it. But the modern evangelical perception of self-esteem has little to do with essential perspective. Though the two are related, how I *see* myself is very different from what I *think* about myself, the root of self-esteem.

Essential perspective is my personal conviction of who I am as a Christian, to the world and to God. It is the most basic belief I possess about what it means to be a Christian in the world. My essential perspective is "essential" because it

will actually determine whether the worldview I seek to formulate is in fact "biblical." If my essential perspective is
wrong, my "biblical worldview" will be little more than an
interesting intellectual concept—encrusted with biblical
language yet devoid of any penetrating influence in my personal life and that of those around me, particularly the rising
generation. For this reason, let's discuss one half of essential
perspective, our identity in relation to the world. In the next
chapter we will explore the final half, our identity in relation
to God.

"In the World, But Not of the World"— Words or Reality?

By tradition and history, the church has opted for a
theological rather than a practical understanding of the truths
that underlie the first half of essential perspective. Most of
the discussion on any topic resembling essential perspective
has rallied under the banner "in the world but not of the
world." Theologians have sought to relieve some of the ten-
sion created by passages like:

> Do not be yoked together with unbelievers. For what do righ-
> teousness and wickedness have in common? Or what fellowship
> can light have with darkness? "Therefore, come out from
> among them and be separate," says the Lord. (2 Cor. 6:14, 17)

> Do not conform any longer to the pattern of this world, but be
> transformed by the renewing of your mind. Then you will be
> able to test and approve what God's will is—his good, pleas-
> ing and perfect will. (Romans 12:2)

These passages seem to contradict Jesus' prayer for His
followers:

> My prayer is not that you take them out of the world but that
> you protect them from the evil one. They are not of the world,
> even as I am not of it. Sanctify them by the truth; your word is
> truth. As you sent me into the world, I have sent them into the

world. For them I sanctify myself, that they too may be truly sanctified. My prayer is not for them alone. I pray also for those who will believe in me through their message. (John 17:15-20)

These Scriptures and others teach that spiritually I am "in Christ," yet experientially I am "in the world." The popular resolution of this apparent conflict has been the cliché-become-doctrine that Christians are "in the world but not of it." Unfortunately, what should be a theological cornerstone has become little more than a speed bump that misdirects our gaze toward the issue of where we are and away from who we are. A solidly biblical grasp of who you and I are as Christians in relation to the world is crucial to a vital faith. Yet this concept has been castrated of clarity and influence in the twentieth century. If it is not purified and restored to biblical wholeness, all the books and seminars on worldview that are beginning to emerge from evangelicalism will, I fear, be a waste of paper and breath.

The Word of God provides us with two clear models of our identity in the world. The modern American church furnishes us with an unfortunate third.

ILLEGITIMATE NATIVES?

The first and by far the clearest model in Scripture is the "native" or "resident." This person is "of the world" in the truest sense of the word. He sees "the world" as place to live, and he also has a permanent attachment to it. But more important, natives are comfortably "at home" in the world. They fit in and feel like they belong. In order to better understand this paradigm, we should understand what the "world" is and what it means to be "at home" in it.

THE KOSMOS

"The world," the phrase that we Christians banter around in our intramural theological musings, comes from the Greek word *kosmos*. In the New Testament, the kosmos can refer to the human race in general, because we are told that "God so loved the *kosmos* that he gave his one and only Son."[1] It is also used to refer to the physical planet, the earth, in 2 Peter 3:6, "By these waters also the world (*kosmos*) of that time was deluged and destroyed." But the more prevalent usage for kosmos in Scripture describes an attitude toward God that excludes Him completely from life. The kosmos has been described by one scholar as "human society organizing itself without God."[2] The story of the Tower of Babel in the Old Testament is an excellent example of human society seeking to organize itself apart from God.[3] The Bible also informs us that the kosmos hates Jesus and those who belong to Him. It cannot know God. The kosmos has its own distinct worldview that is contrary—even hostile—to God.[4] The kosmos is under the control of the evil one, Satan. God tells us further that those who are of the kosmos are controlled by their own desires, led by their own judgments, and bolstered by their own accomplishments.[5] They are, in short, driven and steered by what the Scripture calls "the flesh" (KJV) or "the sinful nature" (NIV).

THIS PRESENT AGE

Those who embrace the identity of a "native" are also "at home" in the kosmos. They feel at home because their vision is limited to a narrow period of time the Bible calls "this present age" (Greek = *aion*). Jesus warned His followers in the parable of the soils that a preoccupation with the present age will stifle spiritual vitality: "The one who received the seed that fell among the thorns is the man who hears the word, but the worries of this life [*aion*] and the deceitfulness of wealth choke it, making it unfruitful" (Matthew 13:22). Elsewhere, God commands Christians not to let this present age "shape us into its mold"[6] and warns us that Satan is the "god of this age (*aion*)."[7]

This "present age" is the time frame to which those of the kosmos—those who are opposed to God—have riveted their passions. This is both a preoccupation with the present and a compelling conviction that the only meaningful life is one lived apart from the purposes and rule of God, a life of genuine autonomy. I believe that Judas Iscariot was a "native." He disregarded the lordship of Jesus Christ in every area of his life, from his petty thievery of the group's money to his final act of high treason. He could not see beyond this present age and was driven by a desire to orchestrate his own life. And as is always the case, what he had hoped would be the sound of sweet harmony degenerated into discord and chaos in the face of the sovereign plans of God.

In summary, a native is one whose essential perspective is characterized by:

• A sense of "belonging" in the *kosmos*,
• A vision that this present age is permanent, and
• The conviction that earth is a place to live independent of God's rule.

It is absolutely vital that we recognize these earmarks of the "native" because the apostle Paul tells us that such people actually oppose the purposes of God and in fact hate Him.[8] Paul makes a clear and unequivocal pronouncement that the natives of this world do not belong to the Lord.[9] One cannot be a genuine, regenerate Christian and a native at the same time. I cannot belong to a group that claims to worship and serve God and a group that disregards and disdains Him. I cannot be for Him and against Him at the same time.

Even more important, if I am truly reborn of the Spirit —one who has been transformed from the status of a native to a child of God—the option of returning to native status is forever closed to me. As Paul says, "May I never boast except in the cross of our Lord Jesus Christ, through which the world [*kosmos*] has been crucified to me, and I to the world [*kosmo*]" (Galatians 6:14). My connection to the kosmos has been severed. Furthermore, my association with Jesus Christ has made me odious to the natives of this present age.

So what is my proper identity in the world? The Bible describes a second model, which should identify those who have been "crucified" to the kosmos.

UNWELCOME ALIENS?

Hebrews 11 has frequently been christened the "Hall of Faith" because of its praise of the men and women who bravely clung to a vibrant faith in God in the face of incredible opposition and hostility. In fact, in the opening lines of the chapter that follows it, we are exhorted to godliness with the reminder to emulate their lives: "Therefore, since we are surrounded by such a great cloud of witnesses [i.e., those of chapter 11], let us throw off everything that hinders and the sin that so easily entangles, and let us run with perseverance the race marked out for us" (Hebrews 12:1).

These were men and women who knew who they truly were in relation to the kosmos. The writer of Hebrews lauds their understanding of their own identity in the world (their essential perspective): "All these people were still living by faith when they died. They did not receive the things promised; they only saw them and welcomed them from a distance. And they admitted that they were aliens and strangers on earth. People who say such things show that they are looking for a country of their own" (11:13, 14).

These men and women of faith saw themselves as "aliens and strangers" in relation to the kosmos. The Greek words translated "aliens" and "strangers" reveal the true nature and meaning of a biblical essential perspective. One of them appears twice in the apostle Peter's letters, which were first penned to encourage and instruct persecuted Christians in exile, a group well-acquainted with the meaning of the word "alien." This word comes from a root that literally means to "stay for a while in a strange place."[10] The emphasis here is twofold. First, an alien is a stranger in a strange land. A genuine alien should never feel "at home" in the place of his sojourn because, in the truest sense, he does not belong. Jesus Himself addressed this reality in the Upper Room shortly before His own crucifixion. "If you belonged to the world, it would love you as its own. As it is, you do not belong to the world, but I have chosen you out of the world. That is why the world hates you."[11]

Second, an alien recognizes the temporary nature of his/her present domicile—planet Earth. The alien is merely "passing through." The modern bumper sticker "Just Visiting This Planet" is an excellent summary of our alien identity. Although the earth is our temporary location, it must never become our vocation. In the words of Scripture, we should be "looking forward to the city with foundations, whose architect and builder is God."[12]

The apostle Paul illuminates the idea of the alien's essential perspective in his letter to the Philippians. He tells the Christians at Philippi that "our citizenship (*politeuma*) is in heaven."[13] His word "citizenship" comes from a Greek word that has been rendered "a colony of heaven on earth."[14] The church, by God's design, is supposed to be a representative colony of heaven. And as such, it has a specific identity and mission. It also has a characteristic lifestyle that flows from and depends upon its alien identity. Paul tells the Philippians that the way they live should be consistent with one who is an alien residing in a strange land. A form of the word *politeuma* appears in his command "Whatever happens, conduct yourselves in a manner worthy of the gospel of Christ."[15]

Paul basically tells them, "Discharge your obligations as citizens of heaven." They were to live a life that was in agreement with who they were. In other words, aliens—members of the heavenly colony—should live like aliens. They should espouse alien values, pursue alien goals, and live in harmony with the alien mission.

In the same verse, Paul speaks of them "contending as one man for the faith of the gospel." The word he chose for "contending" is from the gladiatorial arena, indicating that their faith and its execution were issues of life and death. Life in "the colony" involves a battle, a battle of worldviews, of values, and perhaps in some cases of life itself. Peter uses this same imagery in his statements to the Christians in exile. "Dear friends, I urge you, as aliens and strangers in the world, to abstain from sinful desires, *which war against your soul*."[16] As aliens, Peter writes, we are engaged in a warfare with the passions of the kosmos.

Make no mistake, living as aliens involves a fight. This should not surprise us, however. Jesus warned those who would call themselves Christians that the world would hate them simply because they were "aliens"; they no longer belonged to the kosmos.[17] He also told them clearly what their purpose was to be. They were to have the same sense of mission that He had, namely to rescue others *out* of the kosmos and then teach them how to live *in* it. While on planet earth, their mission would be to enlarge the kingdom of God, while perpetuating and protecting the truth and values of that kingdom.

Paul amplifies this motif in his letter to the young pastor Timothy. "Endure hardship with us like a good soldier of Christ Jesus. *No one serving as a soldier gets involved in civilian affairs*—he wants to please his commanding officer"[18] (emphasis added). Becoming entangled with the kosmos was seen as a serious threat to the alien army of God in the first century. Why would it be any different in the twentieth? It distracts us from our mission and tempts us towards treason.

Such was the case with Demas, a young disciple of Paul's. Although he had been with Paul during a difficult time of the ministry,[19] he lost sight of his alien status and defected to the kosmos. At the end of Paul's life, he wrote these brief but poignant words, "Demas, because he loved this world [*aion*], has deserted me and has gone to Thessalonica."[20] In contrast to these words is Peter's profound response to Christ's query as to whether the disciples would defect to the kosmos. A great number of the Lord's "followers" had decided to trade in their alien status for something more comfortable. Jesus asked the twelve disciples if they were planning to do the same. Peter's answer was the confession of a true alien, "Lord, to whom shall we go? You have the words of eternal life."[21] Peter saw no options. A genuine alien realizes, as Paul did, that the bridges have been burned. There is no place else to go.

True aliens should also have no plans to invest in the system of the kosmos any more than they would in a city at which they spend a holiday. They realize that they are sojourners in a land to which they no longer belong. Aliens must not feel at home in the kosmos, though they remain interested in the people of the kosmos. Jesus' driving passion was people. Those of us who populate the colony of heaven on earth must live for the same reason. To live for any other mission is to fail to discharge our duties as citizens of heaven.

To the degree that we do not encounter opposition to our values, lifestyle, and purposes, to that same degree we are entangled in the kosmos and have forgotten that we are citizens of another place. Perhaps some of us have already gone the way of Demas and deserted the alien colony because of our infatuation with and attachment to this present age. Losing sight of our alien identity is the first step to abandoning our commitment to true discipleship and to the Lord Himself. This is especially crucial for the American church. For in our continued attempts to make the gospel "attractive" and "relevant" to the people of the kosmos, we are increasingly seeking to be like the world rather than distinct and different, the watermark of authentic faith. While they are looking for something unique and genuine, we are flaunting similarities and accommodation.

I spoke once at a family conference about Christians being an alien colony of heaven on earth. At the conclusion of the week, I passed out little plastic aliens that the guests were to keep in their pockets, hang from their rear view mirrors, or place on their desks at work, to remind themselves who they are in the world as Christians. Since then I have received impressive correspondence from several in attendance. Their letters center on the same idea: now that they see themselves as aliens, they want to protect and nurture their alien status. For some, it is becoming a basis for making choices, determining their purpose, and living their lives. When we see ourselves as temporary residents of earth—and as those who are here "on assignment" from heaven—it will impact what we do with our time, our resources, our entire life.

Seeing ourselves as aliens and choosing to live as one is no trifling matter. It will affect our immediate environment, but it is also crucial for the health and survival of the American church. Consider the following statement from Stanley Hauerwas and William Willimon in their provocative book about maintaining the Christian faith in a secular society, *Resident Aliens*:

> A colony is a beachhead, an outpost, an island of one culture in the middle of another, a place where the values of home are reiterated and passed on to the young, a place where the distinctive language and life-style of the resident aliens are lovingly nurtured and reinforced. . . .We believe it is the nature of the church, at any time and in any situation, to be a colony. Perhaps it sounds a bit overly dramatic to describe the actual churches you know as colonies in the midst of an alien culture. But we believe that things have changed for the church residing in America and that faithfulness to Christ demands that *we* either change or else go the way of all compromised forms of the Christian faith. [emphasis in original][22]

The primary change for the "church residing in America" is that she has forgotten her identity in relation to the world. American Christianity has sold her birthright for a bowl of the kosmos. We have abandoned our unique identity and sought to adopt one that we cannot rightfully own—that of the native. Unfortunately, in the process, we have created a third identity that has no legitimate connection to either of the other two—a tourist! And this is our anemic legacy to the rising generation of Christian youth.

"TOURISTS": PILGRIMS WITHOUT A PURPOSE

In either lacking or abandoning a clear understanding of its true alien identity, the American church has forged a new personality that has been described as a "tourist" by James Davison Hunter in his book *Evangelicalism: The Coming Generation.*[23] I agree with his assessment and am convinced that this has become the preeminent identity of the adult sector of the American church. Indeed, our tourist mentality may explain why, worldwide, the Western church seems the most impotent and stagnant.

Tourists are aliens without a purpose. They are opportunists who have forgotten both the temporary nature of their present domicile and their place of origin. Tourists see the world as a place to "play"; a place to maximize one's experience. Tourists see God as a means to personal power and happiness rather than a Lord to be honored and served. Tourists have no genuine allegiance to either the place they are visiting (kosmos) or the place of their citizenship (heaven). Tourists love the kosmos but are indifferent to the people of the kosmos. And, sadly, tourists are usually very offensive to the natives.

Tourists are neither aliens nor natives, yet want to convince both that they belong. In our attempt to be in two worlds at once, we have fallen headlong into a trap that God repeatedly addresses in His Word:

> But if serving the Lord seems undesirable to you, *then choose for yourselves this day whom you will serve,* whether the gods your forefathers served beyond the River, or the gods of the Amorites, in whose land you are living. But as for me and my household, we will serve the Lord." (Joshua 24:15)

Elijah went before the people and said, *"How long will you waver between two opinions? If the Lord is God, follow him; but if Baal is God, follow him."* But the people said nothing. (1 Kings 18:21; emphasis added)

So, because you are lukewarm—neither hot nor cold—I am about to spit you out of my mouth. (Revelation 3:16)

God's people throughout history have repeatedly tried to have it both ways—to be aliens and part of the kosmos—a sort of "kosmic alien"! But there is no place for tourists in the kingdom of God. The mission of the heavenly colony does not allow entanglement with the kosmos, and being a child of God doesn't allow for a return to that which has been "crucified" to us.

Before we can view all of life through the grid of Scripture—cultivate a biblical worldview—we must first view ourselves as aliens in the mirror of the kosmos. Our citizenship is in heaven. Our outpost is on earth. We are to hate the kosmos yet love the natives, not the other way around. If, as you conclude this chapter, you realize that you are more of a tourist than an alien, then cultivating the alien aspect of a biblical essential perspective must become your priority over developing a biblical worldview. Otherwise it will be a mere matter of the mind rather than of the heart.

The rising generation of Christian youth, like those of the sixties, see the shallow and empty nature of our tourist essential perspective. I fear that in rightfully rejecting it, they will also discard the genuine faith that it has perverted. We must begin afresh to cultivate and propagate the alien nature of the Christian faith both individually and corporately. But, in order to do that, we will also have to change the way we see ourselves in relation to God Himself.

NOTES

1. John 3:16.
2. William Barclay, *The Gospel of John*, vol. 2 (Philadelphia: Westminster, 1975), p. 185.
3. "Then they said, 'Come, let us build ourselves a city, with a tower that reaches to the heavens, so that we may make a name for ourselves and not be scattered over the face of the whole earth'" (Genesis 11:4).
4. John 7:7; 15:18-19; John 17:25; 1 Corinthians 1:21; 1 John 4:5; 5:19.
5. 1 John 2:15-17.
6. Romans 12:2, Phillips translation.
7. 2 Corinthians 4:4.
8. Romans 8:6-7.
9. Romans 8:9.
10. William F. Arndt and F. Wilbur Gingrich, *A Greek-English Lexicon of the New Testament* (Chicago: U. of Chicago, 1957), p. 631. The word is *parepideemos* and appears in Hebrews 11:13 and 1 Peter 1:1; 2:11.
11. John 15:19.
12. Hebrews 11:10.
13. Philippians 3:20*a*.
14. In their book *Resident Aliens*, Stanley Hauerwas and William H. Willimon attribute this rendering of the Greek word *politeuma* to the Moffatt translation. I am greatly indebted to portions of *Resident Aliens* for many of the thoughts and conclusions I have come to regarding my concept of essential perspective.
15. Philippians 1:27*a*.
16. 1 Peter 2:11.
17. John 15:18-21.
18. 2 Timothy 2:3-4.
19. We know that Demas accompanied Paul to Rome during his first imprisonment, for he is mentioned in Paul's letters to Philemon and the Colossians, which were penned at this time. Demas must have seen Paul's commitment to the gospel and also his dedication to the alien mission. I suppose it is possible that Demas opted for the "good life" because he was well acquainted with the cost of being an alien.
20. 2 Timothy 4:10.
21. John 6:68.
22. Stanley Hauerwas and William H. Willimon, *Resident Aliens* (Nashville: Abingdon, 1989), p. 12.
23. Hunter's book is the subject of chapter 13 of this book. I am indebted to him for the concept of "tourist." Although he does little to develop the idea, his work is an outstanding description of both the characteristics and danger of tourist essential perspective.

But be very careful to keep the commandment and the law that Moses the servant of the Lord gave you: to love the Lord your God, to walk in all his ways, to obey his commands, to hold fast to him and to serve him with all your heart and all your soul.

Joshua, son of Nun

Why do you call me "Lord, Lord," and not do what I say?

Jesus Christ, Son of God

18

THE MASTER'S APPRENTICE

Essential perspective is a two-dimensional reality. In the horizontal dimension, I see myself as an "alien" on a temporary assignment—a Christian weaving a tapestry of human relationships. But there is a second vital dimension to essential perspective, a vertical one. This involves how I see myself in relation to God, first as a human being and then as a Christian—as one depraved before salvation and one reconciled with God afterward. Unfortunately, our misunderstanding of this vital relationship is as damaging as the alien/tourist confusion about our relationship to the kosmos.

DEPRAVED OR SLIGHTLY DAMAGED?

I teach a theology unit to my juniors that lasts ten weeks. It is little more than an introduction to the historic doctrines of God, man, sin, and salvation. As we near the end of the quarter, I inform the class that as we begin to study the doctrine of sin, my goal is to help them see themselves as "lost sinners on a greased pole to Hell." I tell them in no uncertain terms that I want them to see themselves as "damned as damned can be." My rationale, of course, is that one's appreciation for the work of Christ and the majesty of salvation is proportional to their understanding of the heinous nature of sin—their sin. "Cheap grace" can only exist where one fails to see himself totally lost, totally condemned, and totally helpless.

Lest you think that I am a fire-and-brimstone preacher, allow me to finish the story. Over the period of two weeks, we pretty much covered it all: depravity, condemnation, God's wrath, and hell. They understood that they were hopelessly damned by virtue not only of what they had done, but also of who they were. They were fully convinced that God "doesn't grade on a curve," and that His standard is 100 percent righteousness, nothing less. They rightly saw that man's relative "goodness," though somewhat measurable, did not meet God's holy standard of righteousness any more than a bright light can match the radiance of the noonday sun.

Then, we moved on to study and discuss the glorious truths of salvation: God's holy anger was turned away from them when it was poured out on Jesus in the atonement. God has declared us "not guilty" and given us the righteousness of His own Son, the very thing we needed and lacked. We have been adopted into God's family and are rightfully His children. We have been "branded" with the mark of ownership, God's Holy Spirit, who also is the "earnest money" of God's promise to complete His work of our salvation.

About halfway through the first week of our discussion on salvation, one young lady blurted out in tears, "Mr. Sciacca, why hasn't my youth pastor told me all of this?" I wish I could have captured that moment on film! It had finally dawned on her what it meant to be a Christian because she was overwhelmed with what had happened at Calvary.

I fear that the American church has lost sight of one of the basic tenets of our faith: we are Christians not because we want to be but because we have to be. We are lost, totally lost, apart from the atoning work of Jesus Christ in history. In neglecting this vital truth, we have fallen into the same trap as the church in Laodicea:

To the angel of the church in Laodicea write: These are
the words of the Amen, the faithful and true witness, the ruler
of God's creation. I know your deeds, that you are neither cold
nor hot. I wish you were either one or the other! So, because
you are lukewarm—neither hot nor cold—I am about to spit
you out of my mouth. You say, "I am rich; I have acquired
wealth and do not need a thing." But you do not realize that
you are wretched, pitiful, poor, blind and naked. I counsel
you to buy from me gold refined in the fire, so you can become
rich; and white clothes to wear, so you can cover your shame-
ful nakedness; and salve to put on your eyes, so you can see.
(Revelation 3:14-18)

Ours is an era when talk of depravity and condemnation
is the "mortal sin" of Protestantism. These doctrines are
considered the shackles of the ghost of Evangelicalism Past.
Unfortunately, in severing ourselves from the painful acquaintance with these "archaic" and "negative" notions in
favor of our "massage theology," we have also excised the
only basis we have for fueling the passion for God. True biblical maturity demands that I see more and more of my own
sin and how great the chasm is between me and "the glory of
God."[1] As the gap widens, so does my appreciation for the
one thing that spans it—the cross of Christ.

The young lady in my class that day, part of the church
in America, voiced in exasperation her desire to know what
is already clear in Scripture. Her plea is a sad caricature of
the American church. We have lost sight of the majesty of
our redemption because we are no longer acquainted with
the depth of our depravity. We have bartered the leg of the
historic doctrines of sin and judgment for one that provides
a sense of well-being. Unfortunately, it doesn't fit well, and
without the proper balance we now find ourselves walking
unevenly, wondering who we are and why life seems so difficult. And as we limp along, we not only have lost sight of
who we are before God as human beings, we also no longer
understand who we are before Him as believers.

UNLIMITED PARTNERS?

A close personal friend is a senior vice-president of a large national securities firm. He has helped me isolate an ideal paradigm for understanding the modern Christian's relationship with God. We're part of a "limited partnership." Although no illustration is without weaknesses, this one works very well.

A limited partnership is an investment vehicle that creates a "partnership" between two parties based purely on profit and tax benefits. In the words of my friend, "It is an investment arrangement that provides substantial benefit with little or no risk because the general partner [other person] provides all of the expertise, does all of the work, and takes all of the liability if there is a loss." While it is true that the limited partner (us) puts up most of the capital, the arrangement is weighted so that we also enjoy a larger portion of the benefits at the front end. In short, a limited partnership allows me to be the obvious beneficiary of an arrangement that requires little, if any, work on my part.

Somewhere in the misty past of our theological heritage, God's job description as Lord of the Universe was abandoned in favor of becoming the "general partner" in a growing multitude of relationships with those who call themselves by His name.

This shift has redefined the Christian faith in America. What was once understood as the watermark of authentic faith—an intimate relationship with God—is now perceived in terms of a limited partnership. Being a Christian is now understood more in terms of its benefits than its cost, emphasizing God's "responsibilities" more than our own. Discerning God's will is reduced to merely finding what His thoughts are about my plans. Sanctification is understood as self-improvement; holiness as morality; evangelism as example. The classical notions of submission to the sovereign will of God, self-abasement, conformity to the character of

Jesus Christ, and courageous preaching of the gospel message have gone the way of the pump organ and knickers.

Notably, my friend said he has had to rethink his whole philosophy about limited partnerships, because they tend to stimulate his clients to "exercise their greed glands" once they have seen the profit power they possess. Perhaps we too have exercised our "greed glands" in regard to our relationship with the one who bought us. We need to come to terms with a different perspective on who we are as Christians, one more in harmony with the Word of God.

THE CALL OF THE RABBI

Jesus expresses the true nature of our relationship with God—redeemed sinners—as He instructs anyone who would be His disciple:

> "Come, *follow me*," Jesus said, "and I will make you fishers of men." At once they left their nets and followed him. Going on from there, he saw two other brothers, James son of Zebedee and his brother John. They were in a boat with their father Zebedee, preparing their nets. Jesus called them. . . . (Matthew 4:19-21)

> As he walked along, he saw Levi, son of Alphaeus, sitting at the tax collector's booth. *"Follow me,"* Jesus told him, and Levi got up and followed him. (Mark 2:14)

> The next day Jesus decided to leave for Galilee. Finding Philip, he said to him, *"Follow me."* (John 1:43; emphases added)

More than twenty times in the gospels, Jesus issues the same command, "Follow me."[2] He never extends an invitation to simply join His group or be part of a "ministry team." His invitation is to follow, that is, to place oneself in a subordinate role to His leadership. Jesus' call to the people was typical of the call of any rabbi of His day. It was the call to apprenticeship; the invitation to learn from a Master. And apprenticeship, then as now, always had the same goal: to become like the Master under which one is studying. The proper way to see myself before God as a Christian is as an "apprentice," not a partner.

As I begin to see myself as an apprentice, the roles that constitute my relationship with God recover their proper place. He is the superior party, not merely a "silent partner." I am the subordinate, the learner. Instead of a preoccupation with the benefits of the relationship, I become riveted on its purpose—progress towards the goal of knowing Jesus Christ Himself. His character, His values, His habits, and His passions are to become my own. Conformity to His image, not to the kosmos, becomes my passion. And this is not the optional prerogative of a select few, it is the express will of God for all His children. "For those God foreknew he also *predestined to be conformed to the likeness of his Son*, that he might be the firstborn among many brothers" (Romans 8:29). As Paul told the Corinthian believers, "And we, who with unveiled faces all reflect the Lord's glory, are being *transformed into his likeness* with ever-increasing glory, which comes from the Lord, who is the Spirit" (2 Corinthians 3:18; emphases added).

By defining our relationship with God as a limited partnership rather than an apprenticeship, and by living our lives in relationship to the world as tourists rather than aliens, we have perverted the one thing that is crucial to cultivating and perpetuating a biblical worldview—our essential perspective. We must see ourselves as "alien apprentices" rather than tourists in a limited partnership with God; otherwise, nothing will change. In fact things will only get worse —Christians will read books and attend seminars on worldview, only to return home as educated tourists. And the rising generation will continue to be at risk, perhaps even lost.

What is needed? Individual and corporate lives of the adult generation must undergo a reformation. Nothing less will do. And the proper starting place is our weak grasp of God's Word and our distorted views of true spirituality.

NOTES

1. Romans 3:23. Unfortunately, we readily quote this verse to others in the process of evangelism, and rarely quote it to ourselves as a reminder of from whence we have come!

2. Matthew 4:19; 8:22; 9:9; 10:38; 16:24: 19:21; Mark 1:17; 2:14; 8:34; 10:21; Luke 5:27; 9:23, 59; 14:27; 18:22; John 1:43; 10:27; 12:26; 21:19, 22.

We have done almost everything that is possible with these Hebrew and Greek writings. We have overlaid them, clause by clause, with exhaustive commentaries; we have translated them, revised the translations, and quarreled over the revisions; we have discussed the authenticity and inspiration, and suggested textual history with the aid of colored type; we have mechanically divided the whole into chapters and verses, and sought texts to memorize and quote; we have epitomized into handbooks and extracted school lessons. . . . There is yet one thing left to do with the Bible: simply to read it.

Richard Moulton,
A Short Introduction to the
Literature of the Bible

Christians who have good theological understanding should be able to arrive at conclusions different from those arising out of ungodly beliefs. Yet, millions of Americans who claim to be born again show no signs of having a different moral and intellectual perspective than Americans in general. Unthoughtful attitudes involving such matters as government, education, culture, sexual morality, abortion, and so on suggest that Christians have not learned to make the right connections between piety and reason, between acknowledging the Lordship of Christ and working out the implications of God's Word for all of life.

Herbert Schlossberg
and Marvin Olasky,
Turning Point: A Christian
Worldview Declaration

19

A STRONGER GRIP, A SHARPER FOCUS

Evangelical Christians believe the Bible is the Word of God. It occupies a central place in our theology, worship, organizations, and dialogue. The Bible has launched more missions, forged more speeches, framed more church constitutions, and occupied more shelves than any other book in history.

The Bible is a best-seller in every sense of the word. There are hundreds of varieties in print. The average evangelical home probably has at least five Bibles. There are revised Bibles, student Bibles, "New" Bibles, and chronological Bibles. There are children's, working women's, large-print, micro-print, single-column, multi-column, multi-version, and ultra-thin Bibles. We bind them in leather, eel-skin, Kivar, cloth, and paper. They come on audio cassettes, floppy disks, and video tapes. They appear illustrated, multicolored, in red-letter, and as comic books. Recently, one firm released a Nintendo game, "Bible Adventures," that makes the bold promise to "revolutionize Bible study for the next generation."[1] There is even a condensed Bible, although thankfully it has not been received warmly. (Perhaps the publishers could repackage it as a "lite" Bible, for people who want 25 percent less Scripture!)

Judging by the volume of paper and ink dedicated to the marketing, publication, and distribution of the Word of God, one would expect the evangelical church to be virtually speaking Scripture. Unfortunately, that is not the case. The sobering truth is that more and more Christians know less and less of the Bible. A recent survey found that 22 percent of the Christians responding thought the Bible contained a "Book of Thomas," whereas another 13 percent thought it might contain such a book; more Christians than nonbelievers thought that "God helps those who help themselves" was a verse from the Bible; fewer than one of five Christians read their Bible on a daily basis.[2]

We have become second hand scholars, parroting the ideas of our favorite Christian author, radio ministry, or pastor, while our own Bibles occupy space on our shelves rather than in our hearts and minds. Although vicarious learning is a valid means of becoming acquainted with the Bible, it can become a dangerous counterfeit of true biblical literacy. It gives God's Word little more than a two-finger grasp on our lives. It leaves us at the mercy of personal judgment and third-party "experts." It produces an illusion of familiarity and is far from what God desires and expects. Consider these biblical imperatives:

> Fix these words of mine in your hearts and minds; tie them as symbols on your hands and bind them on your foreheads. (Deuteronomy 11:18)

> Let the word of Christ dwell in you richly as you teach and admonish one another with all wisdom, and as you sing psalms, hymns and spiritual songs with gratitude in your hearts to God. (Colossians 3:16)

> Do your best to present yourself to God as one approved, a workman who does not need to be ashamed and who correctly handles the word of truth. (2 Timothy 2:15)

> I have hidden your word in my heart that I might not sin against you. (Psalm 119:11)

God expects His people to *know* what He has said. The Bible is the clearest and most thorough exposition man has about God, himself, and human history. It tells us who God is, what He is like, and what He expects. The Bible is intended to give us more than just a "to do" list. In fact, misunderstanding this point is largely responsible for our ignorance on the whole issue of worldview. "We learn to be faithful by being obedient to God's Word and by understanding that the Bible teaches not only what we are to do and not to do, but also provides a framework of understanding—a worldview," explain Schlossberg and Olasky.[3]

The Bible stands as a constant reminder and rebuke to man when his perspective on reality is inadequate or wrong. The Bible gives man an "outside word" about the nature and purpose of life. For instance, God declares to His people: "As the heavens are higher than the earth, so are my ways higher than your ways and my thoughts than your thoughts" (Isaiah 55:9). Jesus gave us a warning about faulty perspective during one conversation with Peter:

> Jesus began to speak plainly to his disciples about going to Jerusalem, and what would happen to him there. . . . But Peter took him aside to remonstrate with him. "Heaven forbid, sir," he said. "This is not going to happen to you!" Jesus turned on Peter and said, "Get away from me, you Satan! You are a dangerous trap to me. *You are thinking merely from a human point of view, and not from God's."* (Matthew 16:21-23, The Living Bible; emphasis added)

"The fear of the Lord is the beginning of wisdom"[4] is more than a pithy saying. It is a powerful statement from God about the nature of truth. God is the author of life and the sovereign director of human history. What God says is not merely some type of optional "religious truth," as secular society insists; it is "true truth," as Francis Schaeffer so memorably emphasized.[5]

The revealed Word of God represents true information about all of life. But more important, it represents a comprehensive framework from which to make sense of life. When we reduce the Bible to mere lists of prohibitions and endorsements, we completely disregard the more essential truth that the Bible is a record and exposition of *God's worldview.* God's desire is that His worldview become ours. The Bible must be the vital core of our lives, not merely a lifeless appendage. There are tragic consequences of failure to see this distinction:

> Although we now commonly assert that the Bible provides the standard for every area of life, we rarely make it become the standard. That's partly because we don't always obey the truth that we know, but partly also because we do not know how to use Biblical beliefs to make judgments about what we read in the newspaper every morning, hear at work or school during the day, and watch on television at night.[6]

Even when the Bible (and Bible commentaries, dictionaries, etc.) occupies a large portion of our brains, we must guard against being a sort of cerebral prisoner, isolated from the day-to-day affairs of life in the real world. For many, its influence has been confined to the spiritual "compartment" of our lives. We read books about the Bible, listen to evangelical celebrities preach from the Bible, and believe we are committed to the Bible, but ultimately our outlook is the product of our affiliation with society, not of our relationship with God. The inevitable result, of course, is a secular worldview paired with a sacred vocabulary.

In the final analysis, although we verbally affirm our allegiance to Scripture, we tend to deny it by the way we think and act—which is no different from the world around us. This behavior is related to our second error, a secularized spirituality.

A MISTAKEN STANDARD OF SPITITUALITY

The church has struggled since its inception for a reliable indicator of spiritual vitality and health. We crave some tangible and measurable evidence of our own spirituality and demand it of others in the faith. We have formulated creeds, fractured fellowships, and founded denominations over what we think it means to be truly spiritual. Unfortunately, the majority of our prescriptions for spiritual health have centered on either orthodoxy (right teaching), orthopraxy (right living), or a combination of both.

Doctrine can be articulated and analyzed, and lifestyles are observable and open to scrutiny. Although it is accurate to affirm that God places a premium on theological integrity and godly character, it is equally true that He does so within the larger context of a more crucial ingredient: spiritual passion. Consider the following passages:

> This is what the Lord says: "Let not the wise man boast of his wisdom or the strong man boast of his strength or the rich man boast of his riches, but let him who boasts boast about this: that he understands and knows me, that I am the Lord, who exercises kindness, justice and righteousness on earth, for in these I delight, declares the Lord." (Jeremiah 9:23)

> Jesus replied: "Love the Lord your God with all your heart and with all your soul and with all your mind." (Matthew 22:37)

> I know your deeds, your hard work and your perseverance. I know that you cannot tolerate wicked men, that you have tested those who claim to be apostles but are not, and have found them false. You have persevered and have endured hardships for my name, and have not grown weary. Yet I hold this against you: You have forsaken your first love. (Revelation 2:2-4)

Even our Lord, when probing for the true level of commitment within cowardly Peter, placed devotion before duty, in this memorable exchange:

> When they had finished eating, Jesus said to Simon Peter, "Simon son of John, do you truly love me [devotion] more than these?"

"Yes, Lord," he said, "you know that I love you."
Jesus said, "Feed my lambs [duty]." (John 21:15)

God places a higher premium on *our love for Him* than
He does on our theology, sense of duty, or lifestyle. Certainly,
without a proper understanding of who God is (theology)
and a commitment to do what He asks (lifestyle), our passion
for Him is merely sentimental. But to infer that purity of
doctrine and lifestyle indicates passion for God is equally erroneous. In fact, it is dangerous.

This false idea of spirituality helps explain the spiritual
schizophrenia I observed in many of my students. Parents
who believe that the goal of all Christian education is proper
Christian behavior, rather than biblical values, will be content with children who "don't smoke, don't chew, and don't
date girls that do." In other words, if their children demon-
strate appropriate behavior and are familiar with the content of the Bible, they are assumed to be in good spiritual
health. Yet, because they do not have a distinctly biblical
worldview, their values and their lifestyle are merely products of the surrounding culture rather than of Scripture.
What is desperately needed within evangelicalism today is a
renaissance of authentic piety.

Piety does not mean an exclusive faith characterized by
its distance from the corrupting influences of the world. We
need a rekindling of deep reverence and love for God, with a
view toward personal holiness as outlined in the Bible. For
while the modern church is speaking more *accurately* about
God, thanks to the efforts of the Christian publishing industry, it is also speaking less *affectionately* about Him. This, I
believe, is one of the unfortunate side-effects of viewing myself as a "limited partner" with God. Spirituality is now understood in terms of *my* agenda rather than God's.

This limited partnership motif also accommodates and
enables our preoccupation with self and self-improvement.
The soul's gaze is inward rather than heavenward. Donald
Bloesch, in his classic book *The Crisis of Piety*, addresses the

connection between the demise of true piety and our interest in the self:

> The new interest in counseling and group dynamics in our churches and seminaries mirrors an attempt to cope with the crisis of personal faith by encouraging people to turn inwards [??] and discover who they are in relation to their God and neighbor. Yet too often a purely secular psychological perspective supplants a theological, biblical perspective, and our dependence is directed to our own latent powers rather than to the living Savior, Jesus Christ. It can be said that the fascination with psychotherapy in the religious world today reflects the modern cultural emphasis on self-fulfillment as opposed to bearing the cross, the mark of authentic piety.[7]

TRUE PIETY

Bloesch maintains that true piety is impossible within the confines of a secular value system. The level of our detachment from the *things* of this world is one indicator of the genuineness of our spirituality. But he declares that true piety has nothing in common with legalistic pietism, which measures its spiritual health in terms of distance from the *people* of this world:

> Christians will be both spiritual warriors and active participants in the secular world. Their underlying passion will be to uphold the eternal gospel of Jesus Christ, but they are also to have a lively interest in the society in which God has placed them. . . . Christians will live and work in the secular world, but they must take care not to become secularized, that is, preoccupied with the things of this world. They should accept that which is really creative and good in the world as a gift of God, but they must renounce the love of the world, which is the hallmark of secularization. . . . What is proposed here is a holiness in the world, a piety that is to be lived out in the midst of human suffering and dereliction.[8]

If we are in love with the world, then it rather than God is shaping our perspectives, setting our values, and occupying our time and resources. And God says that if that is the case, we do not love Him—regardless of how loudly we insist we do. The apostle John declares, "Do not love the world [kosmos] or anything in the world. If anyone loves the world, the love of the Father is not in him. For everything in the world—the cravings of sinful man, the lust of his eyes and the boasting of what he has and does—comes not from the Father but from the world" (1 John 2:15-16). Jesus adds: "No one can serve two masters. Either he will hate the one and love the other, or he will be devoted to the one and despise the other. You cannot serve both God and money" (Matthew 6:24).

It is no more possible to have a genuine passion for God if our affections are riveted on this life than it is for a man to love his wife if he is sleeping with another woman. Genuine piety is the product of an intimate association with God on His terms, not a partnership on *our* terms.

The corruption of our individual worldviews and the secularization of the corporate church has come from a slow, nearly imperceptible process. The seriousness of the changes showed only after long periods of time. A frog can be boiled to death voluntarily by raising the water temperature slowly over a long period of time. The reason? Its body temperature gradually adjusts to its environment. When its environment becomes too hot, the frog has stayed put too long to escape. The frog simply cannot perceive the gradual changes within its own body. In like manner, we have accommodated our spiritual lives little by little. And now we are on the threshold of disaster.

For a renaissance of personal piety, we must first examine our false notions of spirituality and admit our infatuation and complicity with the culture. Then we must individually choose to cultivate a relationship with God on His terms rather than our own.

The evangelical community has slowly become a subculture of "tourists," lacking a worldview that is distinctly biblical. We have substituted second-hand scholarship for a first-hand encounter with God's Word. Our minds may be full of facts, but they are devoid of larger controlling principles. And we have reduced personal piety to morality—the mere legislation of behavior rather than the total transformation of character and motive. We have lost sight of who we are and why.

We possess the solution for this present generation, now under attack from most sectors of society. Individuals and institutions have failed the rising generation in their own scramble toward life in the fast lane. Drug prevention, sex education, divorce recovery, and suicide prevention programs will certainly assist in mending the broken hearts and lives of our young. But they cannot provide a satisfying answer to the larger questions of life. Only the truth can do that. Only the truth of God, as revealed in the Scriptures and in the life and death of Jesus Christ, has any chance of rehabilitating this generation. God has entrusted this truth and its proclamation to His people—the church. But before the church can begin to reclaim a generation at risk, it must heal itself. That is our first task.

NOTES

1. This ad appeared in *Christianity Today*, April 8, 1991. The computer toy boasts of being a "Mario Bros.® style game" that "promotes education and Bible literacy while providing electrifying adventure." Many of my students don't know 1 Chronicles from 1 Corinthians. However, I have to question the ultimate value of any product that is Nintendo-based. Also, children will naively group this game with all the other adventures, most of which are violent and have nothing to do with Christian values. Imagine the next generation doing Bible study on a Nintendo!

2. George Barna, "Scriptural Ignorance and Biblical Illiteracy," *Christianity Today*, April 23, 1990, special advertising section.

3. Herbert Schlossberg and Marvin Olasky, *Turning Point: A Christian Worldview Declaration* (Westchester, Ill.: Crossway, 1987), p. 108.

4. Proverbs 9:10.

5. See Francis A. Schaeffer, *The God Who Is There* (Downers Grove, Ill.: InterVarsity, 1979). One of Schaeffer's primary objectives was to debunk the myth that religious truth and historical truth were separate. The former was commonly understood to be comprehended by faith, whereas the latter was understood through reason. Schaeffer taught that because God exists and has revealed Himself in propositional revelation (i.e., the Bible), all truth is inherently spiritual because of its origin. Therefore, the truth of the Judeo-Christian Scriptures is not "religious truth," but "true truth" because it is in harmony with the external realities of the universe. Although Schaeffer's ideas were applauded by evangelicals nearly twenty years ago, our present spiritual state shows that few of us realized the significance of what he was trying to say.

6. Schlossberg and Olasky, *Turning Point*, pp. 19-20.

7. Donald Bloesch, *The Crisis of Piety* (Colorado Springs, Colo.: Helmers & Howard, 1988), pp. 28-29.

8. Ibid., pp. 35, 39.

The accommodation we have been speaking of has con-
stantly taken the form of giving in to the humanistic, secu-
lar consensus which is the dominant destructive force of
our day. And if no change in this comes, our opportunity
will be past. Not only will the compromising portion of
evangelicalism go down in collapse, all of us will be carried
down with it.

Francis A. Schaeffer
The Great Evangelical Disaster

We may indeed be approaching midnight. But if there is
hope, it is to be found in a renewed and repentant people
possessed of a moral vision informed by Scripture, respect-
ing of tradition, and committed to the recovery of character.

Charles Colson
Against the Night

20

RECLAIMING THE GENERATION AT RISK

Nearly three thousand years ago, a young shepherd asked a divinely inspired question of timeless relevance: "When the foundations are being destroyed, what can the righteous do?" (Psalm 11:3). There can be little doubt that in America the foundations are crumbling. The enthronement of materialism in the fifties and the collapse of the sixties' attempt to inaugurate a counterculture led to the downward spiral of our secular culture. We have seen the tragic outcome in the form of the present generation—a generation at risk.

But another major reason for the present generation's peril is the absence of an authentic Christian faith on the part of those professing it. Unless those of us within the evangelical church in the United States strain to recapture a vision of our status as "alien apprentices" and rediscover what it means to have an intimate relationship with God on His terms, by the close of this millennium evangelical Christianity may be indistinguishable from the secular culture.

THE BUCK STARTS HERE!

Throughout the Bible, when God sought to communicate with mankind at large or His people in particular, He did it

primarily through the avenues of leadership and authority.
Whether it was the nation of Israel, its surrounding neighbors, the local church, or even the family, God consistently
has utilized those in authority to reach those under authority. Indeed, God often held leaders accountable for the way-
wardness of their followers.[1] It is rare to find God speaking to
any individual for purely personal reasons. On nearly every
occasion, if God appeared or spoke to an individual, He wanted him to carry a message on His behalf to a larger group.
This is best illustrated in the life and ministry of the prophet
Jeremiah.

The parallels between Jeremiah's day and our own are
chilling. The people of God had adopted the same recreational approach to personal holiness that characterizes the
American church today. They busied themselves with building their own private kingdoms, to the neglect of the things
of God. Adultery, theological perversion, and materialism
abounded while personal piety perished. They were self-indul-
gent and autonomous; they demanded that their preachers
(the prophets) preach sermons that made them feel good about
themselves. A number of God's following indictments on the
nation could easily be leveled against the American church:

> My people have committed two sins: They have forsaken me,
> the spring of living water, and have dug their own cisterns,
> broken cisterns that cannot hold water. (Jeremiah 2:13)[2]

> Therefore say to them, "This is the nation that has not obeyed
> the Lord its God or responded to correction. Truth has per-
> ished; it has vanished from their lips." (7:28)

> My people do not know the requirements of the Lord. (8:1)

> Let the prophet who has a dream tell his dream, but let the
> one who has my word speak it faithfully. . . . I am against the
> prophets who steal from one another words supposedly from
> me. (23:28, 30)

In Jeremiah's day, the people of God displayed autonomy, moral relativism, biblical illiteracy, and even immorality among the spiritual leadership. They elevated the words of God's servants above God himself. These sins are timeless indicators of spiritual decay.

In the midst of this moral and spiritual morass, God commissioned Jeremiah to preach faithfully and forcefully to the spiritual leadership of the people of God—particularly to the other prophets, who spoke to the people on behalf of God.

Before the evangelical church in America can begin to reclaim a generation at risk, it must first realize its own predicament, repent, and strain to recover its true spiritual identity and purpose. But in order for this to occur, the leadership within it must issue a clear and unequivocal call to do so, and then provide the necessary instruction and example. Nothing less will do. And this renewal will need to occur as a rock striking a lake casts forth concentric circles: it must begin with the most crucial one, which can then affect the rest of the lake. It must begin in the home. Then it must spread to the church and the parachurch agencies. Finally, its ripples need to reach Christian higher education.

THE CHRISTIAN HOME—THE INNER CIRCLE

We may doubt that we can reclaim an entire generation; however, we certainly can reclaim our own children and their friends. The home is the reasonable starting place for healing in the church. And the most effective and lasting instrument for accomplishing this healing is parental example. We as evangelical parents need to take a serious inventory of our own spiritual lives. Do we have a distinctly biblical worldview? Do we measure our behavior by the standards of Scripture or by the guy next door? Do our children hear us talk about God in a real and personal way, or do they perceive from our conversations that our faith is an impersonal subject to be studied? Are we living out our faith before them as authentic aliens or simply as tourists?

We must ask ourselves other questions. Do our children see us spending time with God in prayer and Bible study or do they merely see us rushing from one religious activity to another? Have our children ever felt the liberty to ask us the tough questions about God's existence, the truth of Christianity, and the future of man? Do our children see us laboring to enlarge the kingdom of God, or seeking to enhance our own kingdoms? Do our children see us collecting "things," or investing in people? Do they believe they have an option?

These are not merely provocative questions. They are penetrating queries into our own spiritual lives, asked of the ones who know us best. I encourage every parent of junior- or senior-high children to spend a half day with your kids privately; ask them these questions about yourself. Assure them that you will not hold them "hostage" to their answers; give them liberty to be honest. They'll tell you what they "see," which incidentally is also what they are going to become someday. (For those who are not parents or are unmarried, this suggestion fits just as well. Simply ask your questions of those who know you best.)

The personal investment and sacrifice required to cultivate a biblical worldview and lifestyle are enormous, but the stakes are high. An entire generation is at risk! Our lives are on the line, and so is the future of the church.

However, any significant and lasting remedy will be extremely costly. Indeed, many adults, Christian or otherwise, find the idea of personal piety unattractive. A friend recently asked me how I intended to conclude this book. When I told him I planned to exhort the church to recapture a commitment to personal holiness, he became very quiet. He finally responded, "Don't you think that's a little legalistic?" I don't think his reply was peculiar. The word *legalism* has achieved the knee-jerk response status within evangelicalism that *censorship* has in the secular culture. I am not advocating legalism in any form. I am arguing for a rekindled vision of devotion—allegiance driven by love. If we truly believe that Christianity is a relationship, not just a religion, then we need to rekindle our love affair with God. For evangelical Christianity to survive, we must instill in our homes a personal and intimate relationship with the God of the Bible, on His terms. But few of us have any idea how to go about fostering such a relationship, which is essential before we can pass it on to our children. Where do we begin?

For most of us in the adult generation, the demands of such radical change are about as appealing as swimming to Europe; it seems too enormous to tackle. But I believe that the necessary first step is not only attainable, it is crucial. We must begin seeing ourselves as "apprentices" rather than partners. And this is a matter of personal desire, nothing more. Desire is the first step in our journey back to biblical identity, worldview, and an authentic faith that can salvage some from the generation at risk. Only God can work the type of change we are seeking, and I must begin by asking Him, begging Him, to change me.

In order to be an apprentice, I must be with the Master, learning from Him, studying Him, seeking to reproduce His life and character. In one of Jesus' post resurrection appearances, He spent some time teaching two men about Himself from the Scriptures. Their response to His instruction should be our first prayer: "And beginning with Moses and all the Prophets, he explained to them what was said in all the Scriptures concerning himself. . . . They asked each other, 'Were not our hearts burning within us while he talked with us on the road and opened the Scriptures to us?'" (Luke 24:27, 32).

In our therapy-focused spirituality, we have become a cloister of "bleeding hearts." We need to beseech God to make us men and women of "burning hearts." We have to admit to God that we have been seeking relief, rest, and resources rather than seeking Him. The necessary first step in being an apprentice is to tell God we *want* to become one.

There are four key ingredients in this alien apprentice-ship program that eventually strengthen our families. Each one depends upon the other.

LEAVING THE CROWD

First, I need to make the time to be alone with God on a regular and frequent basis. One incident in the life of our Lord illustrates the essential nature of this habit of the heart: "Yet the news about him spread all the more, so that crowds of people came to hear him and to be healed of their sicknesses. *But Jesus often withdrew to lonely places and prayed.*" (Luke 5:15, 16; emphasis added.)

Jesus sometimes said no to ministry! In contrast, many of us have developed the habit of putting others ahead of ourselves to the extent that we schedule out of existence our own need to be with the Master. The good is always enemy of the best, and this is especially true in the arena of our time alone with God. Thomas à Kempis's words call us back: "Watch yourself, bestir yourself, admonish yourself; and whatever others may do, never neglect your own soul."[3]

STILLING THE STORM

The second thing we must do is strive to shut out the noise of our lives. The message of the Scripture repeatedly is that God speaks to us in our silence, not in our fury.[4] We live in an era characterized by noise, distractions, and diver-sions. "Noise pollution" is a valid category in the growing list of environmental hazards. Many are the sirens that lure us away from God or simply prevent us from hearing. If I am to be an apprentice of the Master, I will have to order at least some of my life to exclude the noise that robs me of the nour-ishment I need in His presence. This might mean getting up earlier three days each week, or going for a walk rather than playing racquetball with a friend or business associate.

We may need to say no to the multitude of *good* things that often are the most persistent enemies of what is *best*.

Sadly, according to pastor and author Gordon MacDonald, our intimate friends are often the ones who keep us busiest because they have the easiest access into our private worlds.[5] In the Sciacca home, for instance, life reaches hurricane proportions by 6:30 each morning in our feverish attempt to get a teacher and four children fed and out the door by 7:30. The frenetic pace resumes in the evening, remaining until about 9:00, when the children's homework is finished and they are tucked into bed. Consequently, the only time for personal quiet for me is from 5:30 to 6:30 each morning. If I don't spend time with God then, it simply does not happen. I must also stay away from my basement office if I am to meet meaningfully with the Lord in Bible study and prayer.

Your own personal barriers to meaningful communion with God may be different. But whatever it takes, we must create an atmosphere where if God were to speak, we would be able to hear him.

REDUCING MY PASSIONS

The third thing I will need to do is to take whatever steps are necessary to become a man or woman of "few passions."[6] It took me a long time to fully accept the truth that the needs that surround me will always exceed my resources. I "burned out" once at the Christian school simply because I invested more than I had. And bankruptcy in the spiritual department is the most difficult to repair. I know. I've faced the repair. With the rise of Christian social ministries, the explosion of direct-mail marketing tactics, and Christian broadcast media, each of us is inundated daily with needs beyond our means. To truly be an apprentice to the Master, I must determine what *He* wants me to give myself to. The world and the church will loudly and persistently tell you what *they* want from you. But unless it is in harmony with the Master's will, it will be busyness at best and corrosive at worst.

I spend more than fifty hours each week teaching, preparing to teach, counseling, or attending school related events. I have come to terms with what my "passions" can be: my wife, my four children, and my ministry at the school. I simply cannot be a part of the groups in our city committed to stopping pornography, abortion, gay rights, and so on. That is not to say that they shouldn't be somebody's "passion." They just can't be mine. I make clear to my students not only what I can't do, but why. Anyone who wishes to be an apprentice will have to make similar decisions.

FOOD FOR MY SOUL

The fourth ingredient is the heart of the issue. I need to spend time—regular and frequent—in the pages of God's Word. We all seem to know that God's will for our lives is conformity to the likeness of His Son. But few of us take the time to actually study the Son in Scripture. For many of us, God's Word is more a source of solace than sustenance; a place we infrequently run for comfort rather than a place we daily dig for food. God's stirring reminder to a second generation of Jews waiting to enter the Promised Land remains relevant for the modern American church: "He humbled you, causing you to hunger and then feeding you with manna, which neither you nor your fathers had known, to teach you that man does not live on bread alone *but on every word that comes from the mouth of the Lord*" (Deuteronomy 8:3; emphasis added).

We have substituted a diet of high fiber, second-hand scholarship—the writings of men—for the nourishing sustenance of God's Word. This lack of depth is further hidden from sight thanks to our distinctly Christian vocabulary, a sort of shared religious language that creates a convincing illusion of familiarity with God and His word as we talk among ourselves. With a host of clichés and phrases we can delude ourselves and assume that we know God because we are comfortable with others who claim the same.

Fortunately, there are some simple things we can do to know God as a friend through His word. I would suggest, for

starters, that you begin to spend time in God's Word studying the person of Jesus Christ. The gospel of John provides an
excellent portrait of our Lord. In fact, chapters 13-17 contain
an extensive discussion of most of the concepts I introduced
in "Natives, Aliens, or Tourists?" If I really desire to be like
the Master, I need before me an ever-increasing clear mental
image of Him. And the only place to develop such a perception is the four gospels. Take note of Christ's actions and re-
actions, His treatment of people, His values, His priorities,
His prayer life, His vision and passions. Ask questions about
the passage as you read. Pray about the things you read.
Think the passage through, write ideas on paper. Talk about
it with a friend or family member, especially your mate.

Second, you might join in Bible study with someone
else who has a godly discontent over his or her spiritual life.
Together you can study a Bible book, various topical Bible
studies,[7] even a book on theology. Third, you might form a
small group with others who want to study the Bible and
pray. Begin to study God's Word in earnest with saints of
similar vision.

We must rediscover, on an intensely personal level, the
Bible and its author. We must once again become people
who do not boast in their possession, knowledge, or accomplishments, but in their intimacy with God (see Jeremiah
9:23-24). Whatever the method, make it your aim to know intimately from Scripture the one we are to know intimately
in life.

For the generation at risk, the Christian home is the inner circle of life. It is surely the most important influence on
the rising group of Christian youth. The home must become
a "colony of heaven on earth," a godly guild of apprentices to
the Master. I believe this is our foremost calling as Christian
parents and guardians of the next generation. However, God
never intended Christian families to be islands of spirituality. There is a second circle of influence.

THE CHURCH AND THE PARACHURCH

The primary *message* of the church, according to Scripture, is that the world has been reconciled to God through the substitutionary death of Jesus Christ. The central *mission* of the church is to teach, nurture, and be an example, thus leading those who have been reconciled to a state of genuine spiritual maturity. In the words of the apostle Paul:

> It was he who gave some to be apostles, some to be prophets, some to be evangelists, and some to be pastors and teachers, to prepare God's people for works of service, so that the body of Christ may be built up until we all reach unity in the faith and in the knowledge of the Son of God and become mature, attaining to the whole measure of the fullness of Christ. (Ephesians 4:11-13)

Clearly the local church and its various parachurch expressions are to strive to fulfill the plans God has for individual Christians—namely that they be conformed to the likeness of His Son Jesus Christ.[8] Although this certainly involves the alteration of our lifestyles, its primary intent is the gradual transformation of our inner lives to reflect the heart of God himself. The church must always be driven by the vision of changing lives, not increasing numbers.

The Bible defines spiritual growth in terms of Christ-likeness. The title of Thomas à Kempis's devotional classic, *The Imitation of Christ*, summarizes God's intention for each of us. The spiritual life (personal piety) must be at the head of the church's agenda, not the tail, if we are to successfully confront the challenges of a secular society.

The challenge of secularization comes both from without and within. On one hand, a generation of biblically illiterate adults has assimilated a secular worldview and now espouses secular values, lives a secular lifestyle, and is passing this spiritual vacuity on to the next generation. On the other, the church has lost sight of its primary mission. A growing consensus of evangelical leaders perceives the church's essential mission to be social rather than spiritual in nature. They believe the mission mandate is temporal, not eternal. The reclamation of society in the name of Jesus is a noble, perhaps even biblical ideal. There are certainly enough "causes" to which one can give his life—the unborn, the homeless, pornography, anti-Christian bias in education and government, media violence, substance abuse, fragmented families, and the "Third World," to name just some. All serious. All extremely worthy of a Christian's time, efforts, and resources. But none worthy of a Christian's total devotion. That, by design, is to be reserved for God alone. I fear that evangelicalism is slowly becoming a religion driven by social concern instead of spiritual passion. As Charles Colson warns us:

> Today's misspent enthusiasm for political solutions to the moral problems of our culture arises from a distorted view of both politics and spirituality—too low a view of the power of a sovereign God and too high a view of the ability of man. The idea that human systems, reformed by Christian influence, pave the road to the Kingdom—or at least to revival—has the same utopian ring that one finds in Marxist literature. It also ignores the consistent lesson of history that shows that laws are most often reformed as a result of powerful spiritual movements. I know of no case where a spiritual movement was achieved by passing laws.[9]

Sherwood Wirt agrees. "God's causes have replaced God," he says.[10] Our involvement with the world must be a consequence of our intimacy with God. Social activism must be the fruit of spiritual passion. Donald Bloesch maintains that all "service in the world must be grounded in heartfelt devotion to the Savior, Jesus Christ. Ethical action cannot long maintain itself apart from spiritual passion."[11] In other words, devotion to the host of causes must be the consequence of authentic personal piety. I fear that instead it is increasingly perceived as evidence of piety. The result is a church that is becoming more socially active and more spiritually passive at the same time.

It is easy to point a finger at corporate evil and sin. Pointing the same finger at ourselves and other Christians is considered "judging," and therefore prohibited by Scripture. Using this perverted hermeneutic, it can actually appear to be more "spiritual" for me to let you live in sin than to confront you—even though I would be living in sin if I failed to confront society. Somehow, we've come to believe that our noses belong in the lives of those outside the church but not those within it. This convenient but unfortunate theological reversal provides me with a deep sense of spiritual commitment without having to compromise my values or lifestyle or infringe upon yours. I can maintain my "tourist" status and be active in the church at the same time. In short, I become a "secular saint," simultaneously committed and autonomous, a walking contradiction.

These thoughts will surely raise the ire of some who have given their lives to just causes. That is not my intention. But the extent to which such causes are emphasized in some evangelical quarters amounts to a serious deviation from the primary mission of the church—to preach the message of reconciliation to a lost world and nurture the redeemed so that their lives emulate the life of Jesus Christ. The evangelical church is slowly becoming a group of marginally moral people committed to just causes.

Meanwhile, from without, the second groundswell threatening to redefine the church comes from the generation that believes its destiny is to steer the course of a nation—the baby boom. It is no secret that baby boomers are "rediscovering" religion now that they have children.[12] Sunday school classrooms are growing with "boomerangers," the children of boomers. Churches and parachurch organizations are excited. Some have even redesigned their worship services and recruitment tactics to attract as many boomers as they can from the 76 million in this potentially ripe harvest.[13] The baby boom has always got what it wanted; now, as it cries for "religion," we are scrambling to provide it. But there's a catch. The boomers don't want just any religion. Cheryl Russell spells out the terms of this spiritual thirst. By now it shouldn't surprise us that it is defined in terms of "needs":

> Now that the baby boomers are having children, many of them are returning to religious tradition to give their children a set of beliefs. But the generation's new lifestyles mean that it needs something different from religion than its parents do. The baby boomers need reassurance that the unique course they steer through turbulent waters will not harm their families; they need to feel that they are OK in an ever-changing world.[14]

The boomers "need" a religion that will allow them to live their lives according to their own standards and "feel that they are OK" in the process—a religion that will authenticate and enable a life of autonomy and narcissism. That sounds hauntingly similar to our description of the present generation of evangelicals. Will the church provide such an ideological haven? Will the boomers be given the final slice of the American pie—religion—and thereby "have it all"?

The baby boomers—76 million strong—are seeking a religion that will "meet their needs" by allowing them to maintain autonomy and "feel good about themselves" in the process. They have no sense of absolutes in the area of morality or truth; nor do they see the need for any. They are committed to the family—their own family. They want what's "best" (not what's true) for their kids. They are committed to global social issues that do not impinge on their lifestyle. They are hungry for a "Christianized" secular worldview. Meanwhile, the modern evangelicals continue to drift from a distinctly biblical worldview. They know little about cultivating a genuine relationship with God. Many aren't even interested. They are ignorant of biblical truth, or unwilling to apply it. Narcissism pervades their values and lifestyle.

When the two groups meet, which one will accommodate the other ?

For the church to restore its vision, the combined leadership of evangelical churches and parachurch organizations in the United States must reinstate the two mandates of Scripture: evangelism and discipleship. They must be part of the central mission of your congregations, youth groups, campus fellowships, and small groups. There are some difficult yet clear ways in which to accomplish this.

APPRENTICESHIP, NOT MEMBERSHIP

The preaching, teaching, and discipleship programs in our fellowships need to be designed to enable people to get to know God. Christians need to be taught what an "apprentice" is and how to develop intimacy with God in Bible study and prayer. Because prayer is conversational and people know how to talk, we assume they must know how to pray. But Jesus' disciples asked to be taught how to pray. They said, "Lord, teach us to pray, just as John taught his disciples" (Luke 11:1). Pastors and those in leadership need to teach people how to communicate with God, not simply hold "prayer meetings" or "prayer breakfasts." I am convinced that most congregations contain believers who could teach others how to pray. In our day of databases and direct mail, we seem to have lost sight of the fact that prayer is our most important and effective work.

Prayer is not the only weak link in our corporate lives. There also exists a near famine in terms of familiarity with the Bible. This is due more to prolonged abstinence than mere ignorance. According to Wirt, "When we are physically hungry and miss a meal, our appetite becomes ravenous. But if time passes and we receive no spiritual food, we may lose our appetite for it. So the less we hear of God's Word, the less we may feel the need for it. Malnutrition sets in and we cease to care."[15] Believers need to be encouraged to read and study the Bible, and then taught how to do it. Christians need to be shown how to find comfort, guidance, and counsel from the pages of Scripture, both for themselves and for those around them. Our children need to be taught from an early age that the Word of God speaks to their hurts and needs—and that it provides a set of absolutes for all of life.

This is especially true of those in youth ministry. There is a place for Jello sculpting and block-long ice cream sundaes. But increasing numbers of my students are disappointed by the absence of regular and sound Bible teaching in their youth groups. Many youth leaders feel a tremendous burden to "make the Bible relevant" for their kids. This is a serious mistake. Because the Bible is eternal truth, it is always relevant. The problem is that our young people don't know how to understand it. When we focus our teaching on helping our students learn how to read and study the Bible, they discover for themselves that it is relevant.

HAPPY OR HOLY

Our congregations need to hear preaching on the theme of sanctification. We have lived in the warmth of the doctrine of justification by faith long enough. It is a joy to be forgiven, but our redemption didn't end on the cross even though the necessary work was completed there. Paul reminds us: "It is God who works in you to will and to act according to his good purpose," and, "He who began a good work in you will carry it on to completion until the day of Christ Jesus."[16]

God wants to work in our lives, to change us. And the work He desires to do is contrary to the spirit of this age:

> The spirit of this age is one of personal power; the spirit of Christ is one of humility. The spirit of this age is one of ambitious accomplishment; the spirit of Christ is one of poverty. The spirit of this age is one of self-determination; the spirit of Christ is one of abandonment to Divine Providence.[17]

Christians need to hear their pastors preach passionately and persuasively on the subject of sanctification. Jesus said those who "hunger and thirst for righteousness"[18] will be happy and blessed. Being holy must be exalted above being happy.

Church and parachurch leadership must work to simultaneously proclaim the love of God and the holiness of God. Evangelical churches must become known as places that minister to the broken and hurting, yet uphold the unchanging Word of God as their standard. On one hand we must continue to provide ministries for single parents, but on the other hand we must begin to preach unmistakably against adultery and divorce. God wants us to extend compassion to those dying of AIDS, but also to condemn homosexuality for what it is: the sin of sodomy.

SOCIAL CONCERN—FROM THE INSIDE OUT

Churches involved in social causes should carefully instruct their congregations regarding the reason for their involvement as Christians. Questions of human rights are empty issues without a valid basis for human dignity. The Judeo-Christian worldview alone provides a real basis for human dignity; New Age philosophy and secular humanism do not. Christians need to know that similarity of goals does not mean orthodoxy. Many people do the right things for the wrong reasons—or for no reason at all. Evangelicals should be shown that acts of compassion are more than good deeds; activism is more than religious duty. We have a valid reason for what we do: "Our service is not to be confused with humanitarianism, which often takes the form of condescension and social uplift. We view our neighbor not simply as someone in need, but as one for whom Christ died."[19]

The central mission of the church (evangelism and discipleship) must be the heart of our social concern, not merely an appendage. If the evangelical church is going to be involved, it must do so on an informed and exclusive platform. Our commitment must be born out of the passion of God Himself for the poor, the oppressed, and the forsaken—

not out of some emotional plea for help or the good feeling we get from giving.

I would suggest that pastors and youth workers who are calling their people into "social action" do so after they have taken the time to study the Scriptures with them. Show them, if it can be done, what God thinks about this issue. Spend time in Bible study before you take your youth group on a mission trip to Mexico. And plan for how you will use the trip in their personal lives after you return. They must see the trip as a product of their lives, not merely a summer event. They must see that social involvement is the product of their passion for God, a condition of apprenticeship, not merely something that "Christians must do"!

The leaders within the local congregations must call their people back to a life of personal holiness with a tender social conscience. Only that kind of life will simultaneously please God and affect society. As Bloesch writes: "When Christians again place their fear and trust in the living God; when they seek to draw close to the spiritual wellsprings of faith in prayer and devotion; when they seek to imitate their Savior in a life of outgoing loving service to others, then the secular age will pay heed to their gospel."[20]

But the task of training adults and children is not the final frontier needing reformation. Those who teach the ones who lead also have a part to play.

CHRISTIAN HIGHER EDUCATION—THE FINAL CIRCLE

Once the leadership of evangelical church and parachurch ministries kindles the fires of devotion and piety, who will teach them? That is the role of Christian higher education.

Christian colleges and seminaries must labor to train students how to live, not simply how to make a living. In his recent book *Against the Night*, Charles Colson argues that secular educational institutions have degenerated to the place that they educate only for utilitarian purposes. They provide the necessary skills students will need to make money, yet neglect to instill the ability to think deeply about life. Colson maintains that because truth has vanished from the curriculum, utility has become the guiding principle in education.

Unfortunately, I have felt this same pull within Christian education on the high school level. Growing numbers of my students were merely interested in how an A in my class on apologetics would help them get into "the college of their choice," rather than mastering the material so that they could survive spiritually on that secular campus as "alien apprentices."

Christian educators must help our young—the future leaders of evangelicalism—understand Christianity in terms of a comprehensive unity that affects every area of life, especially their personal lives. Our schools and colleges must help our young people master the Word of God: to read it, study it, and apply it. They must disciple our youth to be men and women of prayer more than of prominence.

Seminaries must teach our pastors how to develop programs within their churches that are preventive in nature rather than merely pathological. They must learn how to help those ravaged by life in a fallen world. But they must also know how to break the cycle of sin and failure that characterizes too much of the Christian community in America. Future pastors must be encouraged to proclaim the truth of God's Word with boldness and without fear of rejection. And seminarians must be helped to cultivate a personal relationship with God that is vibrant, deep, and contagious. A professor's learning objectives should include introducing, explaining, and equipping the next generation to live as "alien apprentices." The professor should define a biblical worldview and explain how it works. I urge teachers to create projects, homework, panel discussions, and debates around this idea. Labor to instill in these young minds who they are to the world and to God, and what that means.

The suggestions in this chapter are lofty, idealistic, and difficult. Some will undoubtedly dismiss them as sweeping generalizations and overreactions. Others will see in them an urgency and reality that cannot be ignored. Although I undoubtedly have painted my case with broad strokes from a wide brush, the central issues are real. They are as urgent as the threat of AIDS or national economic collapse. But they are even more significant because how we choose to respond will determine not only the future of a generation at risk, but also that of Christianity in America.

We are confronted with a rising generation that is at risk, largely as a result of forces we helped set in motion. They are endangered. Will they be lost? Will the church repent of its "tourism," dissolve its unlawful partnership mentality, and cultivate a biblical essential perspective and worldview? Significant numbers of evangelical Christians must seek to cultivate and propagate a biblical worldview and fuel a renaissance of personal piety. Will I? Will you?

A young Oriental student decided to mock his elderly teacher. He caught a small bird and cupped it in his hands behind his back. He then approached the sage with this plan in mind: He would ask the old man what he had in his hand. If he answered correctly, he would then ask the teacher if the bird was alive or dead. If the old man said, "Alive," he would crush the bird. If he answered, "Dead," he would release the bird.

Upon approaching the teacher, the young student said, "What do I have in my hand, old man?"

The man responded, "A bird, my son."

"Is he alive or dead, old man?" the boy prodded.

The sage replied, "The answer to that question, my son, is in your hands."

NOTES

1. See Jeremiah 2:8; 5:30-31; 23:9ff.

2. The metaphor of a cistern is significant. For the ancients, the cistern was the source of life for a village or town. It was the way they trapped and stored water. A cracked cistern meant that an entire city's water supply would slowly leak away. In short, it meant death. In these verses, God accuses the Israelites of trying to live without Him.

3. Thomas a' Kempis, *The Imitation of Christ*, translated and with an introduction by Leo Shereley-Price(New York: Dorset Press, 1952), p. 66.

4. See Lamentations 3:25-26; 1 Kings 19:10ff. (God spoke to Elijah in a "still small voice" rather than in the wind, fire, and earthquake.)

5. In his book *Ordering Your Private World* (Nashville: Oliver Nelson, 1985), MacDonald seeks to help people plagued by time demands sort out the "urgent" from the legitimate. I would highly recommend MacDonald's book as a good starting place for those wondering how to "put it all together" in terms of scheduling, etc.

6. I am indebted to Jerry White of the Navigators for this phrase. He spoke to our teachers at the commencement of a school year and emphasized the importance of this principle. I have never forgotten it.

7. The author has written two Bible studies that show how Bible men and women dealt with tough times. The books, inductive Bible studies geared toward application for today, are *To Walk and Not Grow Weary* and *To Run and Not Grow Tired* (both published with NavPress).

8. See Romans 8:28-29; Ephesians 4:15; 2 Corinthians 3:18.

9. Charles Colson, *Kingdoms in Conflict* (Grand Rapids, Mich.: Zondervan/Morrow, 1987), p. 304.

10. Sherwood E. Wirt, *Thirst for God* (Minneapolis: World Wide Publications, 1989), p. 22.

11. Donald Bloesch, *The Crisis of Piety* (Colorado Springs, Colo.: Helmers & Howard, 1988), p. 15.

12. "Baby Boomers Are Finding Religion," *Colorado Springs Gazette Telegraph* (October 27, 1987).

13. See Paula Rinehart, "The Pivotal Generation: Who Will Tap the Latent Idealism of the Baby Boomers?" *Christianity Today*, October 6, 1989, 21-26. Also in this section was a sidebar entitled "A Church for Bored Boomers."

14. Cheryl Russell, *100 Predictions for the Baby Boom* (New York: Plenum Press, 1987), p. 166.

15. Wirt, *Thirst for God*, p. 29.

16. Philippians 1:6; 2:13.

17. Peter Reinhart, quoted by Elizabeth Elliot, *On Asking God Why* (Old Tappan, N.J.: Revell, 1989), p. 122.

18. Matthew 5:6.

19. Bloesch, The Crisis of Piety, p. 41.

20. Ibid., p. 6.

21

EPILOGUE

In describing people's spiritual pilgrimages in this book, I have used terms you may find new, even radically different from your own understanding. Yet it may intrigue you as well, as you decide whether you are a native, alien, or tourist. This chapter is for the natives who have read this book and now begin to question their own spiritual journeys.

Of course, as you read this book you cannot address directly to the author questions that arise. Nor can the author query his readers. Although you may have been able to distill something of my own spiritual pilgrimage and consequent conversion to Christianity from these pages, I have no means to determine your spiritual condition. Some of you, however, probably are confused about the nature of the Christian faith in general, and perhaps what it actually means to be a Christian in particular. The public image of Christianity has been severely tainted by the indiscretions of a variety of those from within its ranks. The larger church, as we have seen, has also been less than diligent in portraying an accurate portrait of authentic faith. If you are confused or disgusted with American Christianity, I cannot fault you. We have not taken our mission seriously. But truth does not exist because of noble people. It is true because of its source.

Therefore, I would like to take a few pages and explain, as best I can, how the Bible portrays an authentic Christian and how a person becomes one. If you are uncertain about your own spiritual status, this may well be the most important chapter in this book and the beginning of an exciting spiritual pilgrimage.

MAN: A CREATURE OF RELATIONSHIPS

We are social beings—creatures of relationship. In fact, the health of a society is merely the sum of the relative health of our individual relationships. We are society. That is why our private lives must have some accountability to those around us. The AIDS epidemic stands as a modern parable, teaching that one's public and private lives are a unity. We are social beings, and the intersection of our social spheres forms the web of society and culture. Denying this truth does not negate it, even though it can unravel the delicate weave of our social fabric. Which it has.

As human beings, we have four essential relationships: with ourselves, with others, with the environment, and with God. In fact, our sense of personal meaning is merely the product of how meaningful these four relationships are. We have attempted to better understand these relationships by studying academic disciplines around them: psychology, sociology, ecology, and theology. But studying *about* these relationships is a poor substitute for *cultivating* them. It is much like teaching a course on "Cooking with Rice" to the residents of Cambodia instead of actually feeding them or teaching them to farm. Information of a vital nature is worthless until it can be used to meet a need. This is especially true in this arena. We crave personal meaning in these four relationships. Unfortunately, all four are severely fractured.

PROBLEMS WITH THE ONE IN THE MIRROR

The enormous interest and involvement in therapy in America indicates that we are having serious difficulty in the relationship with ourselves. Though we profess to be in therapy because of an insensitive spouse, a painful past, a weight problem, and so on, the unavoidable truth is that we are unhappy with the one in the mirror. We cannot get along with the person we are. In the sixties, phrases like "I've got to get my head together" or "I'm searching for myself" were the telltale signs of a generation looking for a place to live peaceably with itself. In the 1990s, we still can't get along with ourselves. We're not happy with who we are, and we don't know why. Modern advertising has turned our dilemma into an industry—promising to provide the missing piece to our existential puzzle. And in desperation, we partake of a host of personal products and services. Our relationship with ourselves is shattered.

WALLS AROUND US ALL

Our relationship with others is ill, too. Increasingly we are becoming a society of technological cave-dwellers. Our obsession with privacy is causing cultural monuments like the neighborhood and the movie theater to disappear into the mists of modernity. With personal Walkman® stereos we can isolate ourselves from those around us. Bus stops, once places of conversation, today are little more than necessary punctuations in an automaton existence.

Civil and domestic unrest remind us daily that man is at war with those around him. The volcanic political conditions of Eastern Europe only serve to reinforce the deep-seated fear we all have that general annihilation is a heartbeat away. Operation Desert Storm forced us all to rethink the idea that man is basically good. The televisions in our homes daily herald news of starvation, war, and a variety of proofs that we are more likely to be cruel than kind. And in the process of being deluged with the world's pain, we have perfected the art of handling statistics yet lost the capacity to feel for the victims. In the words of one statesman, our society has become a body without a soul. Our relationship with others is fractured.

AT WAR WITH NATURE

Global warming, asbestos from our faucets, toxic waste in ground water, and brown clouds on our horizons testify that we are at war with the environment that sustains us. Jacques Ellul has summarized our deepest fear:

> The human being was made to breathe the good air of nature, but what he breathes is an obscure compound of acids and coal tars. He was created for a living environment, but he dwells in a lunar world of stone, cement, asphalt, glass, cast iron and steel. The trees wilt and blanch among the sterile and stone facades. Cats and dogs disappear little by little in the city, going the way of the horse. Only rats and men remain to populate a dead world.[1]

We are afraid. Our relationship with nature is crumbling. And the illusion of mastery over nature, which science has misled us to embrace, is falling with it. But unlike our relationships with ourselves and others, the loss of this third vital connection may cost us our very lives.

COSMIC ORPHANS OR SIGNIFICANT INDIVIDUALS?

Finally, mankind's desire for a place in the cosmos—the conviction that we are more than a sustained biochemical belch, and certainly more than mere molecules—is equally unmet. Under the charade of intelligence, we have "murdered" God. The German philosopher Friedrich Nietzsche prophetically described our culture in the nineteenth century: "Whither is God? I shall tell you. We have killed him— you and I."[2] Modern man has murdered God. Simon and Garfunkel provide at least a partial explanation of how we accomplished this in their classic ballad "The Sound of Silence": "The people bowed and prayed, to the neon God they made. . . ."

We have denied our need for God, believing it to be an insult to our autonomy. That's why Ted Turner can call Christianity a "religion for losers." We want to be "winners," and winners don't "need" religion. So, like little children, we have simply wished God out of existence. Pushed Him aside. Buried Him alive. But, as Os Guinness correctly points out, "In the world without God man is not so much free as overwhelmingly responsible."[3] In other words, if there is no God, man can usurp credit for all that is good in the world. . . but he is also to blame for all that is evil. And more seriously, we become our only hope. In a world where man's relationship with himself is crippled, his relationships with others fractured, and his relationship with nature threatened, placing the burden of cosmic salvation on his shoulders seems a bit short-sighted.

The resurgence of interest in occultism and New Age philosophy are only two among many indicators that we crave a connection to something outside ourselves. Meanwhile, an intellectual elite claims that our "need for God" is an archaic concept bred by weak minds and silly people. Thus Christianity is immediately dismissed as a way to meet our spiritual need. However, if the God of the Bible is in fact a living reality and not just a religious idea, then the abandonment of Judeo-Christian religious truth is more than an error in judgment. It is spiritual suicide.

If Christianity is true—that is, if it accurately defines life as it should be and explains life as we know it—then it should provide true and satisfactory remedies for the four necessary but shattered relationships of mankind.

The ideas and comments in the remainder of this chapter are based on the presupposition that the Bible is a trustworthy historical document and is the very Word of God. I will make no attempt in this book to verify that belief. If you have serious questions about the reliability of the Bible, I would direct your attention to the host of books dedicated to defending the Scriptures.[4]

PUTTING HUMPTY TOGETHER AGAIN

In the face of the nearly monolithic consensus that we are only biological creatures, the Bible makes a bold claim.

Scripture asserts that man's essential nature is not material, but spiritual:

> For who among men knows the thoughts of a man except the man's spirit within him? In the same way no one knows the thoughts of God except the Spirit of God. (The apostle Paul, in 1 Corinthians 2:11)

> The lamp of the Lord searches the spirit of a man; it searches out his inmost being. (Solomon, in Proverbs 20:27)

In other words, because our essential being is spiritual, our relationship with ourselves must also be spiritual in nature. If we seek to repair a spiritual relationship using nonspiritual means (for instance, psychology, success, or prestige), we are doomed to futility from the start. Because man is spiritual, his emotional and physical attributes must be understood in light of this truth. To deny man's spirituality is to deny his essence. And living independent of our spiritual identity makes us ineffective, and our life senseless and destructive.[5]

The Bible also teaches that man's relationship with God must be spiritual. Jesus declares, "God is spirit, and his worshipers must worship in spirit and in truth" (John 4:24). This means that there is immensely more to knowing God than the mere conclusions of my intellect. There is a nonmaterial basis for being rightly related to God. In fact, it is something beyond the scope of my intellect:

> Where is the wise man? Where is the scholar? Where is the philosopher of this age? Has not God made foolish the wisdom of the world? For since in the wisdom of God the world through its wisdom did not know him, God was pleased through the foolishness of what was preached to save those who believe. (The apostle Paul, in 1 Corinthians 1:20, 21)

Man, on his own, cannot reason his way to a right relationship with God. This doesn't mean that Christianity is a mindless religion. Our reason plays a vital role in maintaining our relationship with God.⁶ But God is not intellectually defined or merely rationally known. A relationship with God is spiritual in nature, according to the Bible.

In summary, the Bible teaches that man and God are both spiritual beings and that their spirituality delineates all their relationships. But the Bible says something else about man regarding his spirituality:

> As for you, *you were dead in your transgressions and sins.* (Ephesians 2:1)

> [God] made us alive with Christ even when *we were dead in transgressions*—it is by grace you have been saved. (Ephesians 2:5).

> When you were *dead in your sins* and in the uncircumcision of your sinful nature. . . . (Colossians 2:13; emphases added)

According to Scripture, man is "dead" because of his "sin." The Bible defines sin as any failure on our part to conform to God's holiness in thought, word, deed, or character. In short, God holds man guilty for who he is and what he has done. That is why the Bible can make the sweeping claim that "all have sinned and fall short of the glory of God."⁷ Although it is true that some people may be better than others in terms of relative goodness, none can claim to be holy. Thus *all* have sinned and fall short of the glory of God. One of the consequences of falling short of God's glory is that we are under His holy judgment against sin. We are, in the truest sense, "lost."

However, the *result* of man's sin is nearly as important as sin's reality. Because of sin, man's spirit is "dead" (i.e., unable to function) even though his body is alive. And because man's relationship with himself and God is spiritual in nature, those relationships cannot exist or be maintained in his natural condition. Man cannot be rightly related to himself or to God because his spirit is dead.

The Bible also has a great deal to say about our other two vital relationships—with others and nature. The cause of all human conflict, according to Scripture, is identical to man's conflict with himself and God: "What causes fights and quarrels among you? Don't they come from your desires that battle within you?" (James 4:1).

The Bible teaches that it is our own selfishness that is responsible for the conflicts we have with others. And this is as true for imperialism as for a family spat. Insider trading, federal deceit, adultery, and even war can be traced to our thirst for more and the extent to which we are willing to quench that thirst. Our fractured relationships with others are the product of our own selfish heart, or theirs, or both. This too is sin.

What about man's abuse of the environment? Does the Bible actually address that violated trust too? Indeed. In fact, it does so with alarming candor and accuracy:

> The earth is defiled by its people; they have disobeyed the laws, violated the statutes and broken the everlasting covenant. *Therefore a curse consumes the earth;* its people must bear their guilt. Therefore earth's inhabitants are burned up, and very few are left." (The prophet Isaiah, in Isaiah 24:5-6)

> Hear the word of the Lord, you Israelites, because the Lord has a charge to bring against you who live in the land: "There is no faithfulness, no love, no acknowledgment of God in the land. There is only cursing, lying and murder, stealing and adultery; they break all bounds, and bloodshed follows bloodshed. *Because of this the land mourns, and all who live in it waste away; the beasts of the field and the birds of the air and the fish of the sea are dying.*" (The prophet Hosea, in Hosea 4:1-3; emphases added)

God declares a clear cause and effect connection exists between the sin of people and the deterioration of His creation—the natural environment. The earth is "consumed" and the "beasts of the fields and the birds of the air and the fish of the sea are dying" because of our cursing, lying, murder, stealing, and adultery. Though it may be more comfortable laying the blame for environmental decay at the feet of corporate industry, the Bible indicts all of mankind. In fact, only in the Judeo-Christian Scriptures will you find a valid basis for making environmental protection a *moral* issue.[8] But the Bible is also honest. It says that the human heart, not an industrial chimney, is the culprit when it comes to ecological issues.

I worked for five years as an environmental chemist. I was a part of the early research resulting from the Clean Water Act. We were assigned the three-year task of helping determine reasonable and suitable discharge standards for the treated waste-water from a split-leather tannery in Minnesota. During that time I learned many valuable lessons about environmental protection. But by far the primary one was that pollution is really a product of consumption more than corruption. It is America's passion for more that fuels the industries that pollute. It is our obsession with image that prompts us to drive large inefficient cars, build extravagant homes, and accumulate more goods than we need. How many pairs of shoes are in your closet? Every one of them contributed to the discharge of some leather tannery. Environmental decay is the product of consumption. And we are a consumer society. God says it loudly, "Your world and its inhabitants are dying because of your selfish hearts."

The Bible tells us that each of man's four essential relationships is ruined because of sin. I am incapable of a relationship with God and a satisfying understanding of myself because my spirit is dead. My selfishness is responsible for the broken relationships I have with people near and far. And a selfish heart is at the core of our deteriorating environment. The Bible says that my spirit is dead and my heart is selfish because I am a sinner in fact and in deed. In short, the Bible says that all of man's problems are moral in nature. We are sinners, and our sin threatens to consume us and everything around us.

Our sin also condemns us in the sight of a holy God, who does not wink at sin as though it did not matter. Man is utterly lost, according to the Judeo-Christian Scriptures. And our spiritual lostness is responsible for the decay of all of life as we know it. This is the message of the Bible in regard to man and his relationships. But, it is only half the message.

NOW FOR THE GOOD NEWS

Because our own hearts are selfish and our spirits are dead, it is impossible for man to deliver himself from this dead condition. Unless help comes from outside of mankind, there is no hope. The good news is that God Himself offers to revitalize our spirit. Listen to the Word of God: "I will give you a new heart and put a new spirit in you; I will remove from you your heart of stone and give you a heart of flesh. And I will put my Spirit in you and move you to follow my decrees and be careful to keep my laws (Ezekiel 36:26-27).

God offers to provide us with the very things we lack—a new spirit and a new heart. The God of the Bible recognizes what we lack and offers to give them to mankind. But there is still the issue that prevents us from having them in the first place: our sin. As Isaiah declares, "Surely the arm of the Lord is not too short to save, nor his ear too dull to hear. But *your iniquities have separated you from your God;* your sins have hidden his face from you, so that he will not hear" (Isaiah 59:1-2; emphasis added).

God makes clear that the problem is not with Him. Our condition is not a product of either His unwillingness or impotence. There is a barrier between us and God, one that we have chosen. It's a moral blockade—our sin. What is needed for us to find our way to God is for our sin to be removed. The sin problem is our problem.

But we have already established that we are incapable of doing anything to heal ourselves. If a solution is to be provided, it will have to come from outside mankind.

The "good news" (i.e., the gospel) of Christianity is that God Himself paid the penalty for man's sin through the atoning sacrifice of Jesus Christ, the Son of God, on the cross. Two eyewitnesses of the resurrected Jesus, Peter and Paul, declare this truth:

For Christ died for sins once for all, the righteous for the un-
righteous, to bring you to God. He was put to death in the
body but made alive by the Spirit. (1 Peter 3:18)

But God demonstrates his own love for us in this: While we
were still sinners, Christ died for us. (Romans 5:8)

The promise of God of a new spirit and heart can be fulfilled because Jesus Christ has dealt with the barrier that
keeps us from that promise—our sin. However, God also
created us with a free will. Therefore He must honor our
choices, even when they are contrary to His demands. To do
less would be immoral on His part. Consequently, the sacrifice of Jesus Christ must be accepted as atonement for sins
by individuals through faith; we must acknowledge our need
for and confidence in the sufficiency of Jesus Christ's sacrifice. This is the New Testament definition of faith. It is not
mere assent to a creed or theological formula. Biblical faith
in Jesus Christ involves a commitment of my eternal destiny
into the hands of God Himself on the basis of the finished
work of His Son on my behalf.

This necessary first step is contrary to everything our
culture embodies and is itself the central reason Christianity
is so offensive. It involves humbling ourselves and admitting
both our insufficiency and our dependence—the antitheses
of self-sufficiency and autonomy, the emblems of modern
man.

This is the Christian gospel in brief. The message is neither an emotional high nor an intellectual formula. It is life
itself. For if Jesus Christ died for each of us, our response
should be to live for Him. Thus the secularized Christianity
appearing in America is not only ludicrous, but blasphe-
mous.

Perhaps people who profess to be Christians have kept
you from contemplating the claims of Jesus Christ for yourself. Perhaps you are skeptical that God really cares. If so,
look at the life of Jesus, faithfully recorded in the Scriptures.
Then I urge you to ponder the question Pontius Pilate put to

the Jews of his day nearly 2,000 years ago, for it is the supreme question of all time. It is a question for which you must have an adequate answer:

"What shall I do then, with Jesus who is called Christ?"[9]

NOTES

1. Jacques Ellul, *The Technological Society*, trans. John Wilkinson (New York: Alfred A. Knopf, 1970), p. 321.

2. Quoted in *The Dust of Death*, by Os Guinness (Downers Grove, Ill.: InterVarsity, 1973), p. 22.

3. Ibid.

4. Four books worth reading on the validity of the scriptural record are *Mere Christianity*, by C.S. Lewis; *He Is There and He Is Not Silent*, by Francis Schaeffer; and *More Evidence That Demands a Verdict* and *More Than a Carpenter*, both by Josh McDowell.

5. One can quickly see the ramifications of this truth in the arena of education, ethics, law, and journalism. To deny discussion and instruction of spiritual truth, especially to children, in the name of constitutional integrity is equivalent to denying food to a starving race in the name of nutrition! We are not speaking here of "religious preferences." This is an issue of objective realities.

6. See, for example: 1 Corinthians 2:16; 14:15; 2 Corinthians 3:13-14; 4:4; 10:5; 11:3; Ephesians 4:22-24; Philippians 4:6-8.

7. Romans 3:23; see also: Ecclesiastes 7:20; Isaiah 53:6; 64:6; Jeremiah 2:29.

8. Environmentalists are fighting a losing battle because they have sought to raise the national conscience on environmental issues using inadequate means. One argument is purely pragmatic: "If we don't clean up the environment, we'll all die!" Unless there is proof of immediate danger, however, people will always pursue the pleasure principle over that of self-preservation. A second argument plays to people's emotions of losing our homeland. The classic example was a public service advertisement in which an American Indian is shown paddling a canoe down a heavily polluted river, dodging the tires and beer cans. Near the end of the commercial, the camera zoomed-in for a close-up of the Indian's face to reveal a tear streaming down his cheek. With all due respect to the Native American heritage and its noted history of preservation (my mother is half Indian), seeing a crying Indian will not compel any selfish individual to give up a life of consumption. Francis Schaeffer's work *Pollution and the Death of Man* is an excellent discussion of why only a Judeo-Christian world view can provide a valid basis for environmental protection and preservation.

9. Matthew 27:22.

BIBLIOGRAPHY

Bloesch, Donald. *The Crisis of Piety.* 2d ed. Colorado Springs, Colo.: Helmers & Howard, 1988.

Bloom, Allan. *Closing of the American Mind.* New York: Simon & Schuster, 1987.

Campolo, Anthony. *Who Switched the Price Tags?* Waco, Tex.: Word, 1986.

Collier, Peter, and David Horowitz. *Destructive Generation: Second Thoughts About the Sixties.* New York: Summit, 1989.

Colson, Charles. Against The Night. Ann Arbor, Mich.: Servant, 1989.

_____. *Kingdoms in Conflict.* Grand Rapids, Mich.: Zondervan/Morrow, 1987.

Gabler, Mel, and Norma Gabler. *What Are They Teaching Our Children?* Wheaton, Ill.: Scripture Press, 1985.

Gitlin, Todd. *The Sixties: Years of Hope, Days of Rage.* Toronto: Bantam, 1987.

Gottlieb, Annie. *Do You Believe in Magic?* New York: Time, 1987.

Greene, Bob. *HOMECOMING: When the Soldiers Returned from Vietnam.* New York: G. P. Putnam's Sons, 1989.

Groothuis, Douglas. *Unmasking the New Age.* Downers Grove, Ill.: InterVarsity, 1986.

Guinness, Os. *Encircling Eyes*. Downers Grove, Ill.: InterVarsity, 1974.

———. *The Dust of Death*. Downers Grove, Ill.: InterVarsity, 1973.

Harris, David. *Dreams Die Hard*. New York: St. Martin's/Marek, 1982.

Hauerwas, Stanley, and William H. Willimon, *Resident Aliens*. Nashville: Abingdon, 1989.

Hunter, James D. *Evangelicalism: The Coming Generation*. Chicago: U. of Chicago, 1987.

Johnson, Paul. *Modern Times*. New York: Harper & Row, 1983.

Larson, Bob. *Rock*. Wheaton, Ill.: Tyndale, 1980.

Lasch, Christopher. *The Culture of Narcissism*. New York: W. W. Norton & Co., 1979.

McDowell, Josh, and Dick Day. *Why Wait? What You Need to Know About the Teen Sexuality Crisis*. San Bernardino, Calif.: Here's Life, 1987.

Quebedeaux, Richard. *The Worldly Evangelicals*. New York: Harper & Row, 1978.

Robbins, Cynthia. *Barbie: Thirty Years of America's Doll*. Chicago: Contemporary, 1989.

Rushdoony, Rousas. *Intellectual Schizophrenia*. Phillipsburg, N.J.: Presb. & Ref., 1961.

Russell, Cheryl. *100 Predictions for the Baby Boom*. New York: Plenum, 1987.

Schaeffer, Francis A. *The Church at the End of the Twentieth Century*. Downers Grove, Ill.: InterVarsity, 1970.

Schaeffer, Francis A. *The Great Evangelical Disaster*. Westchester, Ill.: Good News/Crossway, 1984.

———. *The Church Before the Watching World*. Downers Grove, Ill.: InterVarsity, 1971.

Schlossberg, Herbert, and Marvin Olasky. *Turning Point: A Christian Worldview Declaration*. Westchester, Ill.: Crossway, 1987.

Schlossberg, Herbert. *Idols for Destruction*. Nashville, Tenn.: Thomas Nelson, 1983.

Sire, James. *The Universe Next Door*. Downers Grove, Ill.: InterVarsity, 1976.

Stott, John R. W. *Christian Counter-Culture: The Message of the Sermon on the Mount.* Downers Grove, Ill.: InterVarsity, 1979.

Taylor, Derek. *It Was Twenty Years Ago Today.* New York: Simon & Schuster, 1987.

The Rolling Stone Illustrated History of Rock and Roll. New York: Random, 1976.

This Fabulous Century, Volumes 6 and 7. Alexandria, Va.: Time-Life, 1970.

Thomas, Cal. *The Death of Ethics in America.* Waco, Tex.: Word, 1988.

Vitz, Paul C. *Censorship: Evidence of Bias in Our Children's Textbooks.* Ann Arbor, Mich.: Servant, 1986.

Webber, Robert E. *The Secular Saint.* Grand Rapids, Mich.: Zondervan, 1979.

Wirt, Sherwood Eliot. *A Thirst for God.* Minneapolis: World Wide, 1989.

Moody Press, a ministry of the Moody Bible Institute,
is designed for education, evangelization, and edification.
If we may assist you in knowing more about Christ
and the Christian life, please write us without obligation:
Moody Press, c/o MLM, Chicago, Illinois 60610.